THE
PHILANTHROPIC
MIND

SURPRISING DISCOVERIES FROM
CANADA'S TOP PHILANTHROPISTS

CHUCK ENGLISH & MO LIDSKY

First published by Dog Ear Publishing
4011 Vincennes Rd
Indianapolis, IN 46268
www.dogearpublishing.net

ISBN: 978-1-4575-3991-6

This book is printed on acid-free paper.

Printed in the United States of America

Contents

Acknowledgments

We are deeply grateful to our family, friends, colleagues, and associates whose advice, input, and inspiration helped make this book a reality.

First and foremost, our deepest thanks to our wives, Lydia English and Naomi Lidsky, who, aside from reviewing the manuscript, have shown extraordinary support for the time that this project took away from our families. To them, we are incredibly and immeasurably grateful.

A second thank-you to all the philanthropists who took time out of their extraordinarily busy schedules to spend time with us and share their insights and experiences. They include Naomi Azrieli, Shreyas Ajmera, Lawrence Bloomberg, Brendan Calder, Tony Comper, Martin Connell, Sydney Cooper, David Cynamon, Leslie Dan, Aubrey and Marla Dan, Carlo Fidani, James Fleck, Linda Frum, Harry Gorman, Dr. Gerald Halbert, Jay Hennick, Richard W. Ivey, Hal Jackman, Aditya Jha, Donald Johnson, Charles Juravinski, David Kassie, Warren Kimel, Larry Kinlin, Julia Koschitzky, Mark Krembil, Eric Lindros, Joe Lebovic, Kelly Meighen, Gil Palter, Philip Reichmann, Larry Rosen, Gerry Schwartz, Isadore "Issy" Sharp, Gerald Sheff, Seymour Schulich, Honey Sherman, Alex Shnaider, Gary Slaight, Ed and Fran and Sonshine, Eric Sprott, Larry Tanenbaum, and Fred Waks.

A heartfelt thank-you to all those who reviewed early versions of the manuscript and took the time to provide insightful comments—Tessa MacNeil, Howard English, Pam Feldman, Sidura Ludwig, Randy Spiegel, and Michael Lax. We would like to extend a special thank-you to Joe Bitton and Michael Lax, whose guidance and support of this project has helped make it a reality.

We are deeply grateful to the various interns that helped with transcriptions of interviews. Thank you, Lindsey Cormack, Aliza English, Rose Lidsky, Esther Chang, and Brock Warner. Thank you, as well, to Roxanne Mcdonald, whose help in editing and researching has been invaluable.

We are appreciative to those that graciously offered input on the cover design. Thank you, Anne Atcheson; Daniella Bitton; Resa Lax-Litwack; Judi Egelnick; Atara English; Ariella Orner; Jason Pivovitsch; and Tali, Alon, Zvi, and Rachel Wertheimer.

Lastly, we want to express our thanks to all those whose confidence, guidance, and expertise inspired us to start this project and who provided the encouragement and wisdom to complete it. Thank you to David Wm. Brown, Ross Slater, Randal Craig, Ken Wyman, Ruth Zive, Ian Rosmarin, Terry Smith, Steven Shulman, Ted Hart, Simone Joyaux, Tom Ahern, Marc Pitman, Saul Koschitzky, Kate Bahen, Renee Rubinstein, Jeff Silver, David Ulmer, Mark Nusbaum, Ira Gluskin, Moshe Ronen, Janice Kaufmann, Ronitte Friedman, Pauline Pankowski, Barb Babij, and Merle Goldman.

It's amazing what can result from a coffee meeting. Four years ago when we decided to write this book, we would never have imagined the degree to which the project has become part of our lives and the hundreds of conversations it has spawned. We cannot possibly cite—or, for that matter, remember—every person we spoke to or consulted with in the preparation of this book. You can be certain, however, that our gratitude vastly exceeds the space available or our ability to remember. Thank you.

Why the Philanthropic Mind?

To give away money is an easy matter and any man's power. But to decide to whom to give it and how much and when, for what purpose and how, is neither in every man's power nor an easy matter.

—Aristotle

We've all seen it. The news item about someone who has made a very large donation to a hospital or university has become almost commonplace. There's the photo of the philanthropist giving the oversized cheque to representatives of the organization. There is the requisite quote about the gift's impact and how meaningful it is to support the cause.

But what's the real story? How did that donation really come to be? More importantly, how did the donor's attitudes toward philanthropy lead him or her to choose one organization over another? What is the essence of the philanthropic mind?

That's what we sought to discover in the research that is at the heart of this book. We wanted to know more about philanthropists' passions, motivations, defining experiences, likes, dislikes, joys, and challenges. It was clear that the best source of that information was the philanthropists themselves. With that in mind, we conducted in-depth interviews with dozens of Canada's top philanthropists.

Our interviews were comprehensive. We asked all the questions we could think of without crossing the boundaries of appropriateness. We covered motivations, approaches, solicitations, expectations, relationships, decision making, family, and the next generation. Some of what we heard was astounding—even with our combined decades of experience in philanthropy. We left most of our interviews trying desperately to debrief and process the sheer volume of what we had just heard. More than anything, we were almost always inspired.

Distilling hundreds of hours of interviews and then deciding what to present and how to organize it was a daunting task. To be of the greatest value, we chose eighteen topics that we thought would provide true insight and elevate the philanthropic enterprise as a whole.

We believed that a glimpse into the philanthropic mind could be fascinating or valuable to a number of audiences. For fundraisers, it can provide the key to success—for them and the organizations they represent. In fact, Carlo Fidani, one of our interviewees, told us,

> *I would argue that the people who have their hand out, the eighty-six thousand [non-profit organizations in Canada], have to get better at it and understand what will turn on the thoughtful philanthropist and what they're looking for …*

For the professional and lay leaders of organizations, the insights of Canada's top philanthropists can provide a rich understanding of the decision making that could lead to much-needed funding.

For other donors at various stages of their philanthropic careers, the thinking of those we interviewed may be instructive, motivational, and even validating.

Finally, there may be significance for those who are simply curious and thoughtful. Studies in every major country and every major culture have demonstrated that giving is the single-most important value and guiding principle around the world.[1] The reality is that many of our interviewees are accomplished Canadians, and giving has been central to their accomplishments. Whether one is rich, poor, or anything in between, the stories and views of these givers have the potential to be intriguing and inspirational to anyone in any walk of life who simply seeks to somehow make a difference.

Philanthropy All Around Us

We often take for granted that many of society's most basic and important amenities today are the products of philanthropy.

The 911 service in the United States was a project of the Robert Wood Johnson Foundation[2]; yellow fever vaccine was made possible by the Rockefeller Foundation; rocket science was a result of the Guggenheims; the Pap smear (the most successful cancer screening technique in history) was a product of Harkness family's generosity; and among Andrew Carnegie's many other achievements and remarkable legacies (such as insulin to treat diabetes and Sesame Street programing) were libraries for the masses. Even white lines on the sides of roads were first painted using funding from the Dorr Foundation.

There isn't one corner of our world that hasn't been touched and positively impacted by philanthropy.

I

If history repeats itself, and the unexpected always happens,
how incapable must Man be of learning from experience!

—George Bernard Shaw

You Can't Judge the Philanthropist's Playbook by its Cover

Fundraising organizations conduct copious research on the giving history of prospective major donors. Smart fundraisers might want to take those findings with a grain of salt because in the world of philanthropy, history doesn't always repeat itself. A philanthropist's previous contributions can't be relied upon as an accurate predictor of future giving.

It's not unreasonable to assume that a philanthropist who makes a $5 million donation to the Stratford Festival has an interest in theatre or Shakespeare. But if you made that assumption regarding a contribution that Michael and Kelly Meighen made in 2000, you'd be dead wrong. Don't worry. You're not alone. The following item from *Maclean's* magazine had fundraisers from a variety of arts organizations falling over themselves trying to get a meeting with the Meighens.

> *Canada's pre-eminent Shakespeare festival recently won some extraordinary applause from a pair of die-hard fans. Senator Michael Meighen and his wife, Kelly, have given $5 million to the Stratford Festival, the largest donation in its 48-year history. "The festival has always been a part of our lives," says Michael Meighen ...*

—*Maclean's, October 9, 2000*

So, if it wasn't theatre or Shakespeare, what was the motivation for this gift? Here's what Kelly Meighen told us:

> *Okay, it often doesn't have anything to do with the mission of the institution. We made a big commitment to Stratford several years ago now ... You know why? ... I would describe my interests and my passion for Stratford because my mother is from Stratford. I grew up listening to my grandparents talk about [it] and their pride in what their little town had done. I think Stratford is a miracle when you think of where it happened and how it happened. It's something that Canada has done right. It's excellent. We go to the festival, we take our children, we have family moments, which we remember, that our kids remember. So that's, for me, why Stratford.*

This was a gift about family, pride, and being Canadian. But after the gift was made public, Ms. Meighen said, "We got floods of inquiries from arts organizations and from theatre schools all over the world! 'They must be Shakespeare enthusiasts,' they all assumed."

They all assumed incorrectly because what the Meighens gave to Stratford had no bearing on any future giving.

Kelly Meighen

- President, T. R. Meighen Family Foundation
- Board member of Toronto's Centre for Addiction and Mental Health, University of Western Ontario, and other organizations
- Major supporter of the Stratford Shakespearean Festival, Mount Allison University, and numerous other educational and health-related communal and children's causes

For full bio, see page 135

There's another lesson to be learned from the Meighen gift to Stratford. Both the mission statement and the grant criteria of the T. R. Meighen Family Foundation are "to encourage strategic and creative initiatives benefiting youth at risk in the Province of New Brunswick, Southern Ontario, and the Montreal Area." Stratford and at-risk youth are not exactly a match. Kelly Meighen acknowledged that fact, explaining that Stratford was an "organization that was of interest to the family."

The Meighens aren't the only philanthropists who have a foundation with clearly defined giving criteria and a giving history that sometimes extends beyond those criteria. The foundation established by Eric Sprott, for example, has a process for breaking its own rules—albeit within financial limitations. As Eric explained, "All board members can use discretion on certain things for certain amounts. So if it is some friend that has a project, I can just make that decision without going to the board."

The fact that foundations often give outside their wheelhouse can be confusing to those conducting major gifts research. The reasons for making a gift may be very personal or particular, extending well beyond stated guidelines. The difficulty then becomes figuring out whether a giver is a good prospect for an organization. It may be necessary to accept the fact that philanthropy isn't an actuarial science and that determining a philanthropist's motivation requires a different kind of research.

Hal Jackman's gift to the University of Toronto is another example of hidden intent. His $30 million contribution to the Faculty of Liberal Arts could convince many fundraisers that he was someone who could be relied upon to support programs in history, philosophy, or literature. But again, they would be wrong. Here's what Mr. Jackman told us:

> *"They asked me to be chancellor at the University of Toronto, so I gave money to them. I gave it to the humanities, which is not something that I am big on in particular, but they wanted that. They wanted me to do that because they had all kinds of people giving money to business and engineering, but liberal arts and humanities were being ignored."*

Hal Jackman

- Former lieutenant governor of Ontario
- Former chairman of the board, Empire Life Insurance and National Trust
- Former chancellor, University of Toronto
- Member and officer, Order of Canada
- Benefactor of the Jackman Humanities Institute at University of Toronto and supporter of numerous arts, health-related, and communal causes

For full bio, see page 131

This was a gift motivated by Jackman's deep feeling for the institution. It was certainly noble of him to give money where it was needed as opposed to where his interests lay. However, anyone looking for his support of the humanities at another institution would have been disappointed.

Here's another example from the educational sector. By 1995, Seymour Schulich had established himself as an extremely successful businessman, approaching the billionaire distinction he holds today. It would have made sense that his $15 million gift to create the Schulich School of Business at York University was an expression of his belief in the value of educating future businesspeople. If you were a fundraiser at another Canadian university with a business school waiting to be named, you might have thought you had it made. In fact, you would have been surprised to discover that the business school part of the pitch was a nonstarter. Having named one business school, Schulich wasn't going to do another.

There were, however, nine university benefactions that followed, each exceeding $20 million and each in support of a different academic discipline—law, music, engineering, and medicine, for example. Schulich certainly believed in the cause of education, but there was something more at play. He was creating an educational empire. Schulich calls the collection of schools bearing his name a "composite university." He'll only do one benefaction per city because he doesn't want any "brand confusion."

The Schulich brand is reflected in his rigid, four-point system for making benefactions and what he expects from the institutions he supports. While it may seem limiting, he maintains that the Schulich brand helps the university raise money by attracting other donors. In chapter 4, we will demonstrate that he is right.

The point is that it would have taken an in-depth understanding of Schulich's grand educational vision in order for a fundraiser to be successful. And without that insight, a solicitation was doomed to fail.

Seymour Schulich

- Director, Newmont Mining Corporation and chairman of its merchant banking division
- Founder, Schulich Leader Scholarships, a $100M undergraduate STEM scholarship program
- Benefactor of numerous Canadian university faculties, the Schulich Heart Centre at Toronto's Sunnybrook Health Sciences Centre, and various educational institutions
- Member, Order of Canada

For full bio, see page 137

The following example illustrates how the very core of major gift research may lie in discovering how the gift reflects the self-view of the giver.

The Lindros Legacy Research building at the London Health Sciences Centre was established on the strength of a $5 million gift from National Hockey League star Eric Lindros. It was acknowledged in 2008 as "the largest known one-time charitable donation made by a Canadian sports figure."[3] Coming at the end of Lindros's career as a player, one might think that it marked his transition from professional athlete to committed philanthropist. It's a tempting thought, but it has no basis in reality. Lindros set the record straight when he told us, "I wouldn't consider myself a philanthropist … I just consider myself a very fortunate hockey player."

Then why make a very noticeable six-figure gift? Eric explained:

Eric Lindros

- Former professional National Hockey League player
- Benefactor of the Lindros Legacy Research building at the London Health Sciences Centre's (LHSC) University Hospital.
- Supporter of many other charitable causes

For full bio, see page 135

I wrote a cheque to a hospital to help them out with a new building because I got great care there. And I truly loved the doctor—Dr. Fowler—that took care of me all those years. I continue to help them out through the See The Line initiative as the Honorary chair and help with fundraising in support of Dr. Arthur Brown's work in the area of post injury care. That's how I look at it. I just ... I can't describe it further than that.

In other words, this was a one-time deal. Not surprisingly, Lindros received many inquiries from other worthy institutions. How did he respond?

I did what I did, and if there's another way [other than giving money] to help out, then let me know. But you know, I'm done for a while.

Fundraisers approaching Lindros came up empty because he didn't see himself as a philanthropist. His gift was like repaying a debt or was akin to something you do for family. The reality in the Lindros case is that there was no giving opportunity that would have been right for him. He was done.

The lesson learned from all of these examples—and others—is that you can't judge a philanthropist's playbook by its cover. The effectiveness of research based on giving history is limited because the reasons behind the gift are infinitely more important than the fact that it was given.

The Mystery of Why People Donate

For decades, researchers have been dwelling on the question of why philanthropists give.

Academics have conducted thousands of experiments, and in 2011, scholars Rene Bekkers and Pamala Wiepking surveyed over five hundred peer-reviewed articles and studies of philanthropy. These articles were from a wide range of disciplines, including economics, marketing, social psychology, political science, anthropology, and even neurology.[4] Yet virtually every paper on the subject concludes with the researcher being unable to develop a satisfying theory of donor behavior. It reflects a complicated set of motivations not easily summed up in a single formula.[5]

2

Each generation imagines itself to be more intelligent than the one that went before it and wiser than the one that comes after it.

—George Orwell

Generation Matters

Insight into generational perspectives as well as the motivation and expectations of different generations may be the keys to allowing prospective donors to realize their full philanthropic potential.

Carlo Fidani

- Chairman, Orlando Corporation, a property development and management firm
- Benefactor of the Carlo Fidani Peel Regional Cancer Centre in Mississauga and many other health-related causes

For full bio, see page 127

Younger generations of donors approach philanthropy differently. In part, this may be a result of how those from earlier generations were introduced to the world of giving. Carlo Fidani's reminiscence about his grandfather's charity was echoed in many of our interviews.

They were out of workmen who were looking for work, and in '29, he would invite these people in for dinner, and when they left, he would give them two bucks, which was a lot of money in those days.

Direct service, whether it was in the form of feeding the hungry, clothing the poor, volunteering, or door-to-door solicitations, shaped the early experiences of many philanthropists.

Contrast that to the way newer generations are being introduced. In talking about his wife Lynda Haynes' daughter and son, who are in their early thirties, Martin Connell told us this:

Martin Connell

- Founder, Calmeadow, a microfinancing NGO
- Founder (with his wife Linda Haynes), ACE Bakery
- Former Chair, Toronto Community Foundation
- Member, Order of Canada

For full bio, see page 125

We've had them involved in sitting on a couple juries at the Community Foundation evaluating a couple of competitions for awards, so they've had a chance to sort of see how it's done—what goes into it. They sit on our board. They evaluate and participate. We've given them some discretionary resources to allocate … …"

Here's another example of the stark contrast in first giving experiences. We asked both Eric Sprott and his daughter Juliana about their first meaningful philanthropic experience. Eric said,

Eric Sprott and Juliana Sprott

- Eric is the founder of Sprott Asset Management and Sprott Securities Inc. and established the Sprott Foundation
- Juliana is the president of the foundation
- The Sprotts are generous supporters of many educational, communal, and health-related causes

For full bio, see page 141

I gave a couple hundred bucks to Carleton [University] when I wouldn't have been that old, and a couple hundred bucks felt significant at the time. Maybe I made thirty grand a year, and it was my alma mater and I had a good time there too. I don't know if it's meaningful from a money stance. It is meaningful from a spiritual sense.

Juliana's response couldn't possibly have been more different.

For me, my first meaningful philanthropic gift would be when we donated a hybrid refrigerated truck to Food for Life. That was sort of my first undertaking in my role at the Sprott Foundation where I really felt connected to the grantee; I actually led them in the direction of the hybrid truck. They had come to us looking for whatever, a second-rate, beat-up diesel, and I was like, we can do better than this! And I put them in touch with some guy in Boston that sold these trucks, and they took it from there, and that was the first time for me when I was like, oh my god, I'm engaged. I'm engaged with them, and it's a true collaboration.

Appealing to this newer generation is going to require a major gifts approach with a very different understanding of "making a difference." A 2012 research study of 310 next-generation philanthropists in the United States corroborates our findings. This quote from one of their participants helps make the point.

With my grandparents' or even my parents' generation, there is a very hands-off approach to funding, like we write cheques or we give money, but we are separate from the work that is happening. I want to very much be in a relationship to the work that is happening. I don't want to be standing on the sidelines.[6]

It would then appear that younger philanthropists are looking for much more than the satisfaction of providing support. They want to collaborate, to be part of the decision-making process. Garnering their interest will necessitate providing much greater degrees of involvement.

Naomi Azrieli

- President of Canpro Investments
- Chair and CEO of the Azrieli Foundation
- Azrieli Foundation supports initiatives in architecture, design, and the arts; education; Holocaust commemoration and education and Jewish community; and scientific and medical research.

For full bio, see page 123

The evolution of giving in families where philanthropy emanates from a foundation reveals not only different generational perspectives but a different way of doing business. In preparation for assuming a leadership role in the administration of her family's giving, Naomi Azrieli studied the broader family foundation universe. She discovered this common pattern.

First you have the founder who made all the money. And then you have the family, the next generation, who think about what they want to do by sitting around the kitchen table ... And then the third generation usually goes from the kitchen to the boardroom table.

Richard Ivey's account of the development of his family's foundation follows this pattern perfectly but also provides key insights into motivation.

Richard W. Ivey

- Chairman of the board, Ivest Corporation
- Member, Order of Canada
- Past chair of the Canadian Institute for Advanced Research
- Supporter of many educational, communal, and health-related causes

For full bio, see page 130

It is just an evolution. My parents sort of ran the foundation off the kitchen table until the '70s. Then they asked me to join the board when I was twenty-four, and it was still run off the corner of the kitchen table until sometime in the '80s when they took a secretary from the office and designated her full time to run the place. In the early 90s they decided to bring my sisters in, and around that time, I introduced the idea of becoming more focused because I felt like we could accomplish more. We were just writing cheques. We were writing cheques to the United Way, to the hospital, to the university, to the World Wildlife Fund, and we were getting thanks and rapport, but I don't think we were accomplishing anything other than keeping those organizations in business. I felt if we started to focus, we could change the world.

Ed Sonshine

- CEO, RioCan Real Estate Investment Trust
- Director at many Canadian corporations
- Former chair of Mount Sinai Hospital Foundation and other organizations
- Member, Order of Ontario

For full bio, see page 140

So there you have it. Many members of the newest generation of family foundations don't want to (just) write cheques. They want to change the world. Effective fundraisers are going to have to deliver that experience.

There's another fascinating dynamic regarding the postfounder generations of wealthy families. It's what Ed Sonshine referred to as the "dependently wealthy." He explained it this way:

The biggest philanthropists are entrepreneurs who have made their own money because they have the confidence that if they give it away, they can keep making it. But those from the third or fourth generation of money who got it from their grandpa are afraid that it's going to run out.

Issy Sharp

- Founder, Four Seasons Hotels
- Director of many Canadian corporations and board member of numerous nonprofit organizations
- Officer, Order of Canada
- Benefactor of Toronto's Four Seasons Centre for the Performing Arts

For full bio, see page 138

Those from successive generations who didn't earn the family's riches may be less philanthropically inclined because they see wealth as a finite resource. They lack the confidence or motivation to generate wealth and therefore they feel that what they give away cannot be replaced. People in this situation may never be convinced to make a philanthropic gift, or they may just be donors who need more reassurance.

The fact that many next-generation givers are cutting their philanthropic teeth from a seat in the boardroom leads to very different perspectives. For example, the issue of accountability reveals a veritable gulf in generational outlook.

Issy Sharp's attitude on this is very clear.

> *I don't care about how they spend the money [or] what they use it for. They have people who have that expertise. I just say, "Look, I'm just prepared to give the money for what you're telling me about. I don't follow the paper trail."*

It might seem old-fashioned, but this very attitude has made Issy a role model whose virtues were extolled by many other philanthropists we interviewed.

Aubrey and Marla Dan

- Aubrey is founder and president of Dancap Private Equity Inc. and Dancap Productions Inc. and responsible for bringing *Jersey Boys*, *Wicked*, and *West Side Story* to Canada
- Marla is national president of Canadian Hadassah-WIZO (CHW), one of Canada's leading Jewish women's organizations
- Benefactors of the Aubrey & Marla Dan Program for High-Risk Mothers & Babies at Sunnybrook Hospital in Toronto and the Dan Management & Organizational Studies Program

For full bio, see page 126

The generational bookend on accountability is provided by Marla Dan.

> *I think the younger generation has a different connection. They won't just write the cheque no questions asked. They want to know where exactly is it going and what it's going to be there for, how is it going to be managed, how many hands is it touching before it gets to the end.*

Juliana Sprott's views on the same issue matter expose deeper issues.

> *In my generation, I think we are a little bit more disenfranchised. I think we are much less trusting, much more skeptical. And I am not just going to randomly believe that we are going to do the right thing; I need to see it with my own two eyes ...*

There is a cynicism being expressed here that should propel organizations beyond simple accountability. Reports and public relations pieces aren't going to be enough. Next-gen philanthropists need the opportunity to really kick the tires on a giving proposition.

Raising the next generation of givers isn't always simple. With a worldview that is so very different from that of their parents, it may take more than osmosis for a new generation to feel comfortable philanthropically. Smart families like the Meighens are recognizing that their children may need formal training.

> *As far as integrating them, we have a consultant who is working the boys. This woman had sat down with each of them and said, "Okay, we're going to deconstruct. You identify the area you're interested in learning about, and I'm*

going to show you what it is you need to know about the organization, what the checklist is so you are making informed and educated decisions."

It's interesting to note that even with this gap in approach and philosophy, next-generation donors still see great value in their parents' experiences. Respondents in the study previously cited were asked about the importance of influences on learning and developing personal philanthropy. Two out of three of the top responses were "Observations of the philanthropic activities of parents, grandparents, or other family members" and "What parents, grandparents, or other family members taught about philanthropy."

While being sensitive to the generational position of prospective donors, twenty-first-century fundraisers must avoid pitting the new against the old. Rather, they will need a nuanced view that recognizes the uniqueness of each.

Nurturing Generosity

A 2011 study called "Heart of the Donor"[7] explored the relationship between the giving/volunteering behaviour of individuals and their parents. Here is one set of findings.

	Parents Volunteered Frequently	Parents Volunteered Occasionally	Parents Did Not Volunteer
% of Children Volunteering	49%	31%	20%
	Parents Gave $ to Place of Worship *Frequently*	Parents Gave $ to Place of Worship *Occasionally*	Parents Gave $ to Place of Worship *Rarely or Never*
% of Children Giving $ to Their Place of Worship	55%	39%	39%

3

Those who are happiest are those who do the most for others.

—Booker T. Washington

Triggering the Giving Reflex

Philanthropists want to give. In fact, for many philanthropists, it's hard—if not impossible—not to give. When confronted by a person or an organization in need, the philanthropic reflex is to respond. The best way for a fundraiser to activate that reflex is through a face-to-face meeting.

How do philanthropists protect themselves from this compulsion to give? Some erect barriers.

Kelly Meighen advised her son not to visit a charitable organization with a mission outside their foundation's giving priorities. When he did anyway and became sympathetic to their cause, Kelly's reaction was revealing.

> *That's why you don't go. You don't go because it's tough. He said, "They are really nice." I said, "I am sure they are. But I can't know about that." One of the difficult parts of a job like this is that there are so many people out there so committed and working so hard. It's a terrible thing to have to say that I don't want to know about you because if I knew about you, I'd probably fall in love [with your cause], and then where would I be?*

That's a revealing insight that combines both the purity of purpose and the cynicism of experience. She knows that while she will be drawn to the mission and activity of many organizations, she can't say yes to everyone. Her solution to help her stay focused is to keep her distance.

Ed Sonshine concurs. He recognizes his compulsion to give and the trigger that the personal meeting represents. He explained, "If someone comes to my office, they are leaving with a cheque. I don't have a heart to just shoo them away. So I'm very careful about who I see."

For some philanthropists, the giving reflex translates into providing more support than originally requested. When solicited by an organization seeking the funds to provide black youth with a $1,500 grant toward their first year of university, Eric Sprott said:

> *I'm not going to support sending a kid to school with only $1,500 because he'll end up with a bill at the end of the year. He's going to get a student loan, and it will get him nowhere. It gets him in the door to entrapment. I like the cause, but I think [the $1,500 grant] causes more problems than it solves.*

The Sprott Foundation's solution was to provide $5,000 per student and not just for the first year but for four years. For the Sprotts, this was just a logical extension of the reason they give in the first place. "What is the ultimate goal? To assist somebody, not to make a problem for them."

What's even more impressive about this story is that it's not unusual for the Sprotts. Incredibly, they told us, "There are lots of cases when we might do something more than they have asked [us for]. Happens probably 25 percent of the time."

For many of us, philanthropists often assume a larger-than-life quality. We read their names and the details of their giving so often that they take on an iconic character. We forget that they are people—as vulnerable to a sincere request for help as anyone else.

Linda Frum

- Member, Senate of Canada
- Noted journalist and author of two books
- With husband Howard Sokolowski, chaired the 2013 Negev Dinner
- Supporter of numerous educational, communal, and health-related causes

For full bio, see page 128

Linda Frum reminded us of the humanity of the philanthropist when she said, "Well, to be honest, I tend to avoid [face-to-face solicitations]. I don't do a lot of those because I know myself. I'm not good at saying no. So I just can't do it."

The face-to-face solicitation is regarded by most fundraisers as the nirvana of donor engagement. By one expert's estimation, "personal solicitation, done well, can have a 75–80 percent success rate."[8] It might be tempting to attribute that success to the prowess of the fundraiser. Think again. It often has more to do with the inherent nature of the philanthropist.

A personal meeting can often yield more than a monetary benefit. Philanthropists may be as susceptible to a request for advice as a solicitation for funds. Here's an interesting account from Donald Johnson.

> When I get calls and I know they are calling to set up a meeting, I have a standard response, and that is "I would be happy to meet with you as long as it does not cost me any money or time as a volunteer." I know they are either calling to get a donation or to get me involved in the campaign cabinet or in fundraising. Most of them take me up on it. Then their fallback strategy is "Well, I know you're a very busy guy, and you get a lot of charitable donation solicitations, but you are very experienced in fundraising, and we would appreciate any ideas or advice or suggestions you might have on how we can move this campaign forward." I must say I get a lot of visits from people like that.

Donald K. Johnson

- Vice chairman, BMO Nesbitt Burns, and former president, Burns Fry
- Member and officer, Order of Canada
- Leading advocate of legislative reform related to philanthropic giving
- Benefactor of the Donald K. Johnson Eye Centre at Toronto's University Health Network
- Principal supporter of United Way and numerous other educational and health-related causes

For full bio, see page 132

Many philanthropists told us that their time is more precious than their money. So it wouldn't be wise to discount an offer like the one made by Don Johnson. Moreover, the wisdom of someone with his incredible depth of experience in the philanthropic arena could be invaluable. He told us about how he took the time to help one organization get started.

> Last week, [the founder of] Engineers Without Borders came to see me. He said, "I am not expecting you to make a donation or get involved in the campaign, but I would appreciate your advice in building this organization." We had a couple of hours together, and I gave him my suggestions on putting together a campaign cabinet [and] a fundraising council.

Fundraisers have been trained to know that their ultimate goal, other than getting the gift, is the personal solicitation. What they may not have known is just how valuable that meeting can be, given philanthropists' innate impulse to respond and give.

Don't Underestimate People's Desire to Give

Benjamin Franklin, one of the pioneers in developing best practice for philanthropic solicitations, was asked to chair the campaign to build a Presbyterian church in Philadelphia. To the chagrin of the reverend, Franklin declined the chairmanship but offered some simple yet wise words that every fundraiser should take to heart.

> In the first place, I advise you to apply to all of those whom you know will give something, next to those whom you are uncertain whether they will give anything or not and show them the list of those have given, and lastly do not neglect those whom you are sure will give nothing, for then some of them you will be mistaken.[9]

As Franklin wisely identified, don't write off those you think will never support your efforts. With some, you will be pleasantly surprised.

4

*You will face your greatest opposition
when you are closest to your biggest miracle.*

—Shannon L. Alder

Embrace the Demanding Donor

Some philanthropists can be a pain in the butt. They have their formulas, demands, contracts, and prescribed methods of operation. Negotiating a giving agreement can take months, if not years. Some fundraisers may ask whether it's worth putting up with all this nonsense. Based on our interviews, we reply, "You bet it is."

You see, philanthropists become more than funders. They become partners and influencers and the impact of their involvement can be far reaching.

Kelly Meighen characterizes the philanthropist's relationship with the organization this way:

> *You're an investor. You know, you're a partner, so it's time and thought as well as a financial commitment.*

Aubrey Dan is quite clear about what he will demand from the organizations that he and his wife, Marla, will support.

> *I want to make sure the funds get managed properly, and I expect the reports. I want to look at their finances or details. So it isn't just, "Here's the money. Good luck." I want to make sure you're accountable in how you manage it.*

The quid pro quo for him is his active involvement, as exemplified by the Aubrey Dan Program in Management and Organizational Studies at Western University.

I'm still involved with Western, so you may give more of your time and guidance and being there as opposed to just writing the cheque. And that is really what fundraising is about. Yes, you need the money. But you also want some kind of involvement within the organization.

Mark Krembil is just as clear about his expectations from the organizations and initiatives he funds: "In my case, I'm looking for results. I'm not looking to support an institution." But what he offers in exchange—beyond the gift—is perhaps of greater value.

Most of his family foundation's support is for research projects in the health care sector, and his preference is to work directly with the researcher. Therein lies the added value.

I challenge them with questions about what's going on from a perspective that they don't usually see. They only talk to their science colleagues. I hopefully bring a different perspective. So I try to provide value that way. So I see myself as sort of a silent partner with these guys. I try and establish a partnership with each of them.

Carlo Fidani also focuses his giving in the health care sector, but to gain his support, you will have to satisfy his insistence on collaborative projects. He believes that's only fair: "You know, if you push me to give you a gift, that's great; I'm all over that. But what's to say I can't push back?"

Fidani works hard at making philanthropic decisions.

It's easy to give money away, but it's hard to give it away well. And in order to give it away well, you have to work at it like you would a business. You have to research it. You have to understand it. You have to know who your partners are.

There's that word "partners" again, but from Fidani's perspective, it takes on greater proportions.

I want to place my bet where the greatest number of people intersect. It's the greatest collaboration, it's the greatest area of commonality, [greater] area of interest and, if properly engineered, I think a far greater opportunity for success …

And the payoff for meeting his requirements for collaboration? Successful examples of Fidani breaking down silos to bring together medical practitioners and departments are the Joey and Toby Tanenbaum Family Gamma Knife Centre at the University Health Network, as well as the University of Toronto's Terrence Donnelly Health Sciences Complex. These projects also exemplify Fidani's willingness to collaborate with other funders. Fidani explains the impact of this synergy, saying, "So suddenly there is a knock-on effect, and you find that what we started with—two people—could end up being five or six, and they start talking about a bigger picture." It's worth noting that while Fidani was both a driving force and a lead giver on the projects above, neither of them bear his name.

Lawrence Bloomberg is unapologetic for what he demands from organizations he supports.

Lawrence Bloomberg

- Chairman, BloombergSen
- Chancellor, Ryerson University
- Member, Order of Canada
- Benefactor, Bloomberg Faculty of Nursing at the University of Toronto and numerous health, education, and business causes

For full bio, see page 124

We live in a world where accountability has become everything. That can translate into a number of requirements. I mean, sometimes before you make a gift, you'll lay out what metrics, what goals you expect to achieve. In a university, [it might be] the number of graduates that they're going to produce in the faculty, the number of staff in certain areas, the amount of money directed to IT ...

In establishing the Bloomberg Manulife Prize, McGill University reaped the benefit of accommodating Lawrence's exacting approach. He worked with them for more than a year to launch the project using many of his powerful business connections. "I got the *Globe and Mail* as a publishing sponsor. I got WestJet. I am going to get others because I believe this project will likely provide Canadians with greater access to health care," he told us proudly.

Jay Hennick

- Founder and CEO, FirstService Corporation, a real estate development and management firm
- Chairman, Mount. Sinai Hospital, Toronto
- Benefactor of the Hennick Centre of Business and Law at York University and The Jay S. Hennick JD/MBA Program at the University of Ottawa Law School

For full bio, see page 130

For Jay Hennick, there's little glory in philanthropy. As he puts it:

Somebody like me spends a hundred hours a week running my business, so when I hear somebody calling me for money, whatever it is, it's ... my immediate reaction is "This is offensive." This [charitable proposal] is work on my part. I have to wrap my head around something, or not, make a decision, so it is work.

Not surprisingly, Jay maintains that givers have the right to be demanding.

> *Give me a five-year plan. I don't want just numbers. Give me some metrics that you're very comfortable you can exceed, so at least I know we're moving in the right direction. That's what donors should do on larger gifts.*

Brett Wilson described a major gift in which his demands allowed an organization to exceed their own expectations. His family became supporters of a local hospital in recognition of the care and compassion that they provided to his grandmother and mother. The first gift to the hospital was $160,000 to purchase a new x-ray machine. A year later, Wilson contacted the hospital's CEO and asked, "What do you need this year?" The CEO wisely asked Wilson how much he would like to give, to which Wilson coyly responded, "I'm not sure. Come back to me with your ask."

Brett Wilson

- Owner, Prairie Merchant Corporation, and chairman, Canoe Financial
- Benefactor of the Wilson Centre for Entrepreneurial Excellence at the University of Saskatchewan
- Member, Order of Canada

For full bio, see page 143

The CEO was smart enough to provide Wilson with a broad range of giving opportunities. The $600,000 for new anaesthesiology machines caught his eye, but as Wilson said, "I wanted to do more than write a cheque." He picks up the story.

> *I told the hospital I would give $300,000 towards the new machines, but they had to match my donation by raising $300,000 themselves.*

Wilson's condition was more demanding than he realized. He later found out that the most the hospital had ever raised during one campaign was $100,000.

The story gets even better because the hospital accepted the condition but wanted twelve months in which to raise the money. What was Wilson's response? "I thought for a few minutes and gave them three months." The hospital took on the challenge and not only raised the required amount in three months but exceeded their goal with a campaign total of $500,000. Wilson's reaction was remarkable.

> *I was so moved by the way the community had come together, and there was little I could do now but match them dollar for dollar and up my donation to $500,000. The hospital was now sitting on $1 million. To say that they had surprised themselves was an understatement.*

The payoff for meeting Wilson's demand of raising the money in three months was not only $1 million but the heightened profile—and confidence—of the organization.

In the educational arena, Seymour Schulich is likely the most demanding—and one of the most generous donors in Canada. He says that "giving money away is harder than making it," and he passes that difficulty on to the organizations he supports.

Schulich's benefactions all include an exacting four-point plan based in large part on his distrust of university bureaucracies. "Now you want to keep as much [money] away from the goddamn universities as you can—although you can't do it." His solution is this:

Half the money must be used for scholarships.

The other half of the benefaction must be used to establish a dean's super fund that "empowers the faculty leader, subject only to presidential approval, to spend money to upgrade the faculty." In making the last stipulation, Schulich says he is trying to transform deans into "academic entrepreneurs."

The third stipulation is that there must be matching support—either from government or other supporters.

His final requirement is a commitment to improve teaching through granting performance awards that are determined based on the opinions of students.

Why would institutions agree to this daunting formula? Well, for one, his benefactions are in the $15–25 million range. Two, becoming part of the Schulich brand has proven tangible benefits. As an example, both York University's business faculty and Western University's school of medicine witnessed improved empirical performance in the years after Schulich's gift. Student enrollment, faculty size, physical space, and perhaps most importantly, other donations all increased.[10] In fact, the terms of the benefaction at Western were that the school raise an additional $17 million in fifteen years. They did it in three, and in the ten years after Schulich's gift, they raised over $100 million.

That could be why other universities and organizations are clamouring for his support. They recognize that the demands that certainly qualify Schulich—and other similar donors—as demanding are the ones that have the potential to transform an organization.

There Are Limits of Listening to Donors' Demands

In 2011, hedge fund manager Robert Burton gave $3 million to the University of Connecticut Athletic Department. Unfortunately, it was not long before his affection for the program turned into fury and wrath. Why? Burton was apparently infuriated that he was not consulted on the hiring of a new football manager. For such an affront, he demanded immediate return of his $3 million. It took no less than the governor of Connecticut—along with all the executives of the university—to calm the waters. However, the dust didn't settle until the embarrassing spectacle spilled over every corner of local media.[11]

5

It is better to be prepared for an opportunity and not have one,
than to have an opportunity and not be prepared.

—Whitney M. Young Jr.

Timing is Everything

There are times when a fundraiser just has to go for it. You may not yet be at the ideal point in the relationship with the donor or in the perfect setting, but if the right moment presents itself and you don't take advantage, you may be squandering the opportunity for an amazing gift solicitation.

Here's a great example. Ed and Fran Sonshine had been at Mount Sinai Hospital because their eldest grandson had just been born. They were less than impressed with the waiting area in the maternity ward. Some time after, they ran into Joe Mapa, Mount Sinai's CEO, at a gathering and decided to vent. Ed said to him, "Joe, the waiting room in the maternity area is a disgrace. It was dirty. The couches were so filthy that I didn't even want to sit down. I stood for three hours. There wasn't a phone; there wasn't a television that was working." Unfazed by the rant and apparently understanding the power of the moment, Mapa looked at Ed and said, "You know, the government doesn't give us money for stuff like that. Why don't you buy us a new one?" Perhaps sensing what was really happening, the only response that Ed could muster was "What?" So Mapa continued. "Why don't you buy us a new one? Why don't you pay for us to make a nice waiting room? If you want one and if you think it's important, we would love to have a new waiting room." And Ed's final response? "Okay, I'll call the office, and we'll figure out how much it costs."

Fran Sonshine

- Consummate nonprofit leader and volunteer
- National Chair of the Canadian Society for Yad Vashem
- Together with husband Ed, supporter of numerous health-related and communal causes

For full bio, see page 140

Opportunity's reward didn't end there. As Ed explains, their support grew beyond the result of that fortuitous ask.

So the Fran and Ed Sonshine waiting room is now at Mount Sinai, and we're building a whole new wing there—six floors, maternity and women's health. And the waiting room here is going to be twice as big and twice as nice and cost me twice as much. I re-upped.

You might think that philanthropists would feel taken advantage of in these situations. It's not true. If anything, they often appreciate what is a type of gamesmanship in the encounter. The Sonshines recognized Mapa's adroitness and referred to this as one of the "smoothest" asks that had ever been made to them. They admiringly recounted, "It came out of left field, but that was a pretty neat solicitation."

Sometimes, opportunity is represented in pairing an understanding of the donor's background and motives with a unique situation. Warren Kimel tells the story of how their family came to purchase two MRI machines for a major hospital.

> *My father came from Poland looking for a deal. That's just who he is. So the first deal he got was when the hospital came to us and wanted to give us two MRIs for the price of one. What that means, I have no idea. It was a $2.5 million gift, and somebody had donated one MRI but didn't want their name on it, so they could give my father the value of two. Fantastic. The doctor there said to my father, "Mr. Kimel, I know you want a deal. This is the best deal I have. These are very good machines, and nobody has them in the city."*

Warren Kimel

- Chief Executive Officer, Fabricland
- Chair, Baycrest Centre Foundation Board
- Benefactor of the Kimel Education Centre
- Supporter of numerous communal and health-related causes

For full bio, see page 133

The doctor found the perfect way to take advantage of this unique coincidence of one donor's rejection of recognition and another's love of a good deal. He could effectively give credit for both machines to Mr. Kimel. Characterizing a charitable giving opportunity as "this is the best deal I have" would ordinarily have been risky. In this case, however, it was a winning gambit.

Not surprisingly, six months later, the Kimel family's donation of two MRI machines was a done deal.

The Sonshines have another story that demonstrates what can happen when a fundraiser capitalizes on inspiration to create a transformative moment. They were attending a dinner at a building, facing the Western Wall in the Old City of Jerusalem. Ed told us, "I just went out to get a breath of fresh air on the balcony. It was nighttime. The lights [at the Western Wall] were on. The moon was out, shining on the wall. It was spectacular." He and Fran were then joined on the balcony by Richard Rabinowitz, a fundraiser working for the organization that was housed in the building. Ed continues, "I'm not a particularly spiritual person, but I went out there, and I said to Richard, 'You know, it's impossible not to feel spiritual right here. It's impossible—in the centre of thousands of years of Jewish history, seeing this.'" That was apparently all that Rabinowitz needed to hear in order to realize a moment had arrived. He said to Eddie, "You know, in the new part [of the complex] we're building, there's another balcony just like this! It could have your name on it!" Could anyone be surprised at Sonshine's response? "I said, 'Okay … for how much?' And there is now a Sonshine Family balcony there."

Gerald Sheff

- Former CEO and present Chair of Gluskin Sheff and Associates.
- Board member, McGill University, Art Gallery of Ontario, Scotiabank Giller Prize, and the Canadian Centre of Architecture
- Supporter of numerous educational, arts-based, health-related and communal causes

For full bio, see page 138

Seizing these moments is not a matter of coercion. If the philanthropist didn't want to give, he wouldn't. Rather, the fundraiser perceived the presence of a meaningful moment that unleashed the philanthropist's inclination to give.

All that having been said, just because you have the opportunity to make a solicitation doesn't necessarily mean it's a good idea. Gerald Sheff recounts the story of a poorly timed approach that took place in a doctor's office while planning upcoming surgery.

I had been in the hospital with this burst appendix. Anyways, so I am in his office scheduling the surgery. [The doctor and I] only met as a result of this. He doesn't know me, but he knew my name. That's just what happens in hospitals. If they think they have a mark, they pay attention. He is a very nice guy, and he said to me, half apologetically, "I hope you don't mind, I'd like to talk to you about some of our research programs." I said, "Now?!" He said,

"No, after the operation [is fine]." But it was almost like blackmail. "Do you want the A surgery or the B surgery?"

Not only should great fundraisers recognize the moment of opportunity, they need the restraint and judgment to perceive its absence.

A fundraiser's opportunism doesn't always have to be about getting the gift. Rather, it might involve getting the philanthropist to accept the recognition that will lead to other gifts. Brendan Calder was a longtime supporter of the Toronto International Film Festival (TIFF). When they embarked on a campaign to build a new home for the Festival, Calder made a $1 million commitment. His stipulation was "I don't want my name anywhere. I don't want anyone to know it's a million." Recognizing that TIFF was just at the start of a $192 million campaign and that his name on a list could be critical to garnering additional support, he conceded to be listed as a $500,000 donor. But the people at TIFF persisted in wanting to recognize his gift. "They said, 'We need you there. You're going to get this, and you're going to get your name there.'" Calder wasn't buying this, and his answer was clear. "I said, 'I don't need a room. I don't need a balcony. I don't need a named place. I don't need anything. Just put me on the list so I can say, come on, join me there.'"

Brendan Calder

- Former CEO, Chair, and President of CIBC Mortgages
- Director of numerous Canadian corporations
- Founding and principal supporter of the Toronto International Film Festival

For full bio, see page 124

Fast-forward to just before the opening of the new building with Sandy Mackenzie now in charge of the fundraising effort. Just before the first board meeting was to take place in the new facility and a week prior to the official opening, he arranged a private meeting with Calder. Brendan sets the scene.

It's the first time we're having a board meeting in the new place. It's a brand-new board room in a brand-new building. And he says to me, "Brendan, I know philanthropy. I work with philanthropists. You are a true philanthropist. Not only do you give money, but you help get other money, and you put in energy, and you helped build this organization." And then the kicker. He said, "I know you don't want your name on anything, but I just want you to know that we've decided we're going to name this board room the Brendan Calder Board Room—whether you like it or not."

That was quite a risk given Calder's previous insistence on no recognition. What was Brendan's immediate response? "And I'm choking up now." After making sure that the organization's leadership knew about it, Brendan threw in the white flag. "I said, 'You got me.'"

Calder's analysis of the situation is insightful. "So they knew how to get me. So that kind of recognition, it just knocked me out of my socks. It was unsolicited, it was un-negotiated, and the way this guy presented it really did hit me because the nexus of my strengths and my passion is management." It was the perfect recognition pitch at the perfect moment in the perfect place.

James Fleck

- Former CEO, Fleck Manufacturing Inc.
- Professor emeritus, University of Toronto's Rotman School of Business
- President, Art Gallery of Ontario Foundation
- Renowned supporter of the arts as well as many health-related and communal causes
- Officer, Order of Canada

For full bio, see page 128

The final word on opportunism goes to James Fleck, whose extensive involvement in philanthropy has seen him asking for the gift almost as many times as he's been asked. His "Fleck Flinch Test" isn't about finding the right moment for the solicitation but rather about being nimble once the gift request has been made. Here's how it works. Once you have asked a donor to contribute a specific amount, you wait and watch. If the person doesn't flinch, you make it clear that you were asking for that particular amount annually for the next five years. If he does flinch, you explain that the requested gift can of course be spread over five years. The test is more of a paradigm than a playbook. As Fleck says, "Of course, it isn't done quite that way. That's an oversimplification. But you're trying to get a sense."

Perhaps the "sense" that he's referring to is exactly what we're talking about. The honed ability to perceive and act upon the unique convergence of philanthropic inclination and opportunity is what sets the best fundraisers apart from the rest.

If You Only Have One Shot, Don't Squander It

In his later years, as one of the richest men in the world, Henry Ford decided to pay a visit to Ireland and the humble village from which he came. On Ford's arrival, all the excited villagers gathered around him, and one of them blurted out, "Mr. Ford, I'm sure you know that we are about to build a community hospital here in the village. We would appreciate a generous contribution from you." Ford, somewhat astounded by the immediate solicitation, said, "Okay, I'd be pleased to contribute $5,000." And with that, he bid the villagers a good night.

The next morning, the solicitor of the funds came running into the dining room huffing and puffing. "Mr. Ford," he said, "I'm terribly sorry to report that there is a most egregious mistake in this morning's newspaper," whereupon he unfurled the newspaper whose headline read in bold, large letters: HENRY FORD LAUNCHES VILLAGE HOSPITAL CAMPAIGN WITH UNPRECEDENTED GIFT OF $50,000. The flustered villagers watched the stunned Henry Ford read the headline. The villager was quick to say, "Don't worry, Mr. Ford. We intend to print a retraction in bold, equally large print in tomorrow's newspaper!" Ford, having regained his composure, said that was not necessary. Instead, he would honour the $50,000 "pledge."

However, Ford said that he needed the villagers to keep a pledge of their own. The plaque to be unveiled at the hospital's inauguration needed to be prepared by Mr. Ford and not seen by anyone until it was revealed officially at the opening ceremonies. Five years later, that day came. The plaque was uncovered, and it read: "*I came unto you as a stranger and you took me in. Matthew 25:35*"[12]

6

Givers Crave Giving

There's next to nothing that philanthropists would change about their giving history. They have few regrets. They enjoy giving. In fact, they crave giving. Fundraising success hinges on knowing how to satisfy that desire.

There is a purity of purpose that allows most philanthropists to be very sanguine about their giving history. Even though some gifts may not have had the desired impact or, in hindsight, seem ill considered, philanthropists often take solace in the fact that at least they served a philanthropic end. They may also have afforded the philanthropist an opportunity to learn from his or her mistakes. Issy Sharp philosophically sums up this sense of contentment.

> *All the things you've done that worked out and didn't work out, it's all in a basket. And if you could change one thing, for sure the balance of the basket would be different. So I say I had no wish to change because I am satisfied with where it is today. And I know for sure that if I were to change something that might have gone wrong twenty-five or however many years back, then maybe we'd not be where we are today. I don't look upon it as mistakes. I don't look upon them as something that might have been better or worse. I say it's all pulled together as an omelet. You can't take it apart. So I wouldn't change anything.*

Julia Koschitzky

- Lifetime volunteer and philanthropist
- Past chair of the Keren Hayesod World Board of Trustees
- Board member of numerous philanthropic organizations
- With her husband, Henry, supporter of numerous communal, educational and health-related causes

For full bio, see page 134

We tend to think that philanthropists want to get away with giving the smallest gift possible. It's not true. For more than one philanthropist, their only regret was not the decision to give to an organization but whether the gift was large enough. Listen to what Julia Koschitzky had to say:

What keeps me up at night about my philanthropy is not giving enough. I always tell people I'm never sorry that I gave. I'm only sorry that I don't give enough. I never thought that I gave too much.

Not surprisingly, her advice to other donors follows suit.

Don't ask yourself what's the minimum you can get away with. Ask yourself what's the maximum you could give. I think everybody has to ask themself that.

Gil Palter

- Cofounder, EdgeStone Capital Partners
- Founder and former chief executive officer, Eladdan Capital Partners
- Previously recognized as one of Canada's Top 40 under 40
- Supporter of many communal and educational causes

For full bio, see page 136

Gil Palter takes Koschitzky's values-based approach and gives it a self-satisfaction twist.

Every time you give a bigger gift, you feel better, and you realize you could have afforded it all along. So if I could go back with what I know now, I probably would have just given larger gifts earlier along the way. Because it's like wading into the water. You say, "Okay, it's not so cold. I can go deeper. This is actually quite pleasant. I should have just jumped in the first place."

It's possible, if not probable, that by asking a donor to consider a larger gift, you may in fact be doing him or her a favour. You are leading the donor away from the path of regret and to a state of fulfillment. You are accommodating his or her need to give.

There might even be times when donors choose to increase their gifts without being asked. Consider what Senator Linda Frum told us.

> *It has happened from time to time that I have been at events with Howard [Sokolowski], and we'll be there, and he'll say to me, "We didn't give enough money." Because the event is so powerful, he'll go home and write a bigger cheque.*

A proactive fundraiser shouldn't wait for the philanthropist's inner voice to speak. A well-timed call after the event may be what's necessary to capitalize on the philanthropist's vulnerability or inspiration.

For many philanthropists, the most annoying gift solicitations are not ones in which the requested commitment is too large or outside their sphere of interest. What really gets under their skin is when those representing an organization don't ask for a gift.

In talking about excellent fundraisers with whom he has worked, Hal Jackman says, "They are good, and they don't hesitate to ask." In contrast, he told us about his frustrating experience with a dean at the university who had lunch with Jackman several times but could never muster the courage to ask him for a gift. His advice to fundraisers is clear.

> *Be forthcoming. Donors are usually pretty bright people. They are successful business types, and they want to be approached on a business-like basis. They want you to get to the point. If you are trying to sell me some machine tools for my plant, you aren't going to invite me to the opera and do a lot of social things before you make your ask and try to sell.*

He astutely ascribes the solicitor's reticence to a fear of rejection. "People never offended me by asking for money. That's the biggest problem that they have. They don't like asking, but I have no problem saying no, and that is what they don't want to hear."

To be fair, Jackman is quick to point out that some givers fear saying no as much as fundraisers fear hearing that word. "The worst thing donors do is keep [their solicitors] dangling on a string; either say yes or no, and both sides can get on with their business."

Jackman's comments are an example of the sage advice that philanthropists can offer fundraising professionals and fellow donors. The finer point is that the chance to make a personal solicitation to someone like Hal Jackman is rare. Squandering the opportunity is committing a fundraising crime.

Brendan Calder brings that point—and more—to light.

Harry Gorman

- President, Wycliffe International Design Group Chairman
- Supporter of numerous causes including Baycrest, Holland Bloorview, and Toronto General & Western Hospital
- Jewish National Fund Negev Dinner honouree 1995

For full bio, see page 129

The worst ones I've seen, where I let them get near me, are the ones that don't know how to close. They don't know how to ask. They come and present what a good thing this is. I know them, or else they wouldn't have got in the room, but they never do "the ask"! So I end up training them! And I say, "You've got to know how to do 'the ask.'"

It's hard to imagine a philanthropist instructing the solicitor in how to ask for the gift. If that isn't evidence of the proclivity to give, nothing is.

There are times when activating the philanthropist's giving reflex may take extreme measures. This hilarious account from Harry Gorman describes an occasion when he was doing the asking and a peer of his needed to be convinced.

So I said to him, "I want $10,000." He said, "Are you crazy?" I said, "Then I'm going to sit on your desk." I got on his desk, and I sat down, and I said, "I'm not leaving." He said, "I got three guys out there coming for a meeting. You've got to get out of here." I said, "Yeah, when you tell me you're giving me $10,000." He said, "You can't sit there. You're crazy." So I said, "I don't care. Go have your meeting. I'll enjoy listening." He finally said, "Okay, okay, I'll give you the $10,000." I said, "I want it now. I don't want you to tell me you're going to give it to me. I want it today." He told his assistant to go make it up, and I got the $10,000.

It's not an approach that we would recommend, but clearly, Gorman knew that deep down this giver wanted to give.

We commonly view the philanthropist as having the position of power. But the reality is that philanthropists often need the help of the fundraiser. By asking for the gift and pushing the envelope on the size of that gift, fundraisers can help true philanthropists satisfy their natural and very admirable inclination to stretch themselves for a worthy cause.

People Underestimate Generosity of Others

We have a tendency to underestimate how generous people are. Researchers Frank Flynn and Vanessa Bohns demonstrated that this even applies to complete and utter strangers.[13] In one example, study participants in New York City were asked to approach strangers on the street and ask to borrow their cell phones for a call. However, right beforehand, the participants were asked to predict how many of those they approached would comply. They predicted that no more than 30 percent would lend it to them. In fact, 48 percent allowed them to do so.

In a similar study, when approaching strangers, claiming they were lost and asking to be walked to a nearby destination, study participants expected only 14 percent to assist them. In fact, 43 percent did so.

Similarly, when it came to raising money for charity, study participants consistently overestimated how many people they would have to solicit to meet their fundraising goals and at the same time grossly underestimated the average dollar amount that people were willing to give.

Why do we underestimate people's generosity? Flynn and Bohns hypothesize that it is because when predicting the responses of others, we focus on the costs of saying yes and neglect the costs of saying no. As a result of guilt, shame, appearing to be selfish, and so on, it may just be cheaper to say yes.

7

Take egotism out, and you would castrate the benefactor.

—Ralph Waldo Emerson

Major Donors Need Special Treatment

Let's face it. Most donors like, and perhaps even expect, special treatment once they've made a major gift. That could mean something as simple as involving them in decision making. It could be providing front-row seating at an event. Or it could even mean something controversial like allowing them to jump the queue in a health care institution. Anyway you cut it, providing the philanthropist with perks is one of the best ways to cement a relationship.

Offering donors perks is a contentious issue in the fundraising world. For sure, there are many narrow ethical paths to be navigated. At its core, however, it may simply be a matter of competition, as explained by Marla Dan.

> *So from a fundraising perspective, [donors] look at it like there's a lot of competition out there. So if you're not going to treat me [the way I expect] and I'm not going to get [what I want], then I'll take my dollars elsewhere.*

It's not surprising, then, that philanthropists expect to be treated in particular ways once they've made a gift. This is Gil Palter's take on the issue.

> *What is bad is if you are showered with love and treated like an insider until the minute they get your money and then you're ignored afterwards. That's bad. Good is the opposite. Good is being treated with as much love—and I use that word loosely; you know what I mean—that you are kept in the loop about what's going on, that you are consulted about fundamental decisions, that you are treated as an insider.*

David J. Kassie

- Chairman, Canaccord Genuity Group
- Member of the boards of numerous corporations
- Director/trustee of the Hospital for Sick Children and board member and supporter of numerous other educational, arts-based, and health-related causes

For full bio, see page 132

That "insider" treatment has a wide variety of expressions. In talking about the various ways that organizations can express their gratitude, David Kassie said, "You know TIFF [Toronto International Film Festival] is a good one because there's so many ways to thank people. You get to go in a green room with Angelina Jolie and whatever."

The pre-performance reception that provides donors with the exclusive opportunity to meet celebrity guests is a staple of fundraising events. While somewhat controversial, major donors to political campaigns are frequently provided access to government leaders.

In our interviews, preferential treatment in heath care institutions was the most debated issue related to perks. A major tenet of Canada's socialized medical care system is equality of access to medical care. With patients often waiting months for specialized testing like MRIs, granting favoured access can be highly contentious. Nevertheless, our interviews clearly revealed that philanthropists often receive and, in some cases, expect to receive special treatment. In this part of the discussion, we have chosen not to disclose the identities of the individuals quoted and the institutions referenced.

One of the philanthropists described what happened after his family donated an MRI machine to a hospital.

> *And then we get requests—you know, can I get them an MRI? I was so embarrassed, I was like, "How do we do this?" My wife says, "Well, remember they told us if you ever need anything, give us a call." So we phoned up for the first person. I say, "Look, I have a friend, aunt, relative, they need an MRI. Could you do something for me?" "Oh, yeah, no problem—all we need is the request from the doctor, and we'll see what we can do." All of the sudden, two days later, I get a phone call from my aunt, saying, "Thank you so much. I got the MRI." Okay, fantastic. So we were really embarrassed to even ask, and the hospital basically said, "Look, guys, not many people are able to do something like this for the hospital. If you're lucky [and kind] enough to be able to do something for us, we're happy to do something for you."*

This is a clearly expressed quid pro quo. You scratch our back, and we're happy to scratch yours. Not all philanthropists shared that discomfort with asking for this kind of privileged treatment. For some, like the donor quoted below, it's part of an implied contract.

> *I think we're entitled to do it. Because these institutions wouldn't be there today if the major donors in the first instance hadn't [donated]. There wouldn't be a hospital. So it's a two-way street, really. You don't trade on it, but when it's needed, you shouldn't have to go to the back of the queue and wait for fifty people who don't give anything to the hospital to be ahead of you. I think there's nothing wrong with that.*

Those sentiments are the logical preamble to the common view expressed below.

> *It's an insurance policy. Those who treat it like an insurance policy will get more money out of me. It's that simple. It's no different than if you're the lead sponsor for an event. I expect to be sitting in the front.*

One interviewee sees a parallel to the way businesses such as airlines treat their best customers. "Absolutely you get to jump the line. It's called 'express.' We were in Orlando just this past weekend. Express line. Boom. That's the way it is."

Interestingly, however, this individual senses there is a limit to what the donor can expect. "Do I pull that card often? No, because you know that there's psychologically a certain amount in your bank account. You're going to really pick and choose where you want to utilize that."

Many philanthropists seemed to wrestle with the ethical implications of preferred access, wanting to see it as less of an exchange and more as the outgrowth of the relationships that are developed with individuals. Sometimes this resulted in drawing fine lines, as evidenced in these comments.

> *I think that if you're giving money with that [preferred access] as part of the motive, then I think that you're misrepresenting the purpose for which you do it. Do I think that [donors] deserve it? Not necessarily deserve it, but what inevitably happens if you're doing this well, you develop relationships. They return your phone call; they extend their day for you. You twist your ankle at five o'clock, and they will see you when they normally go home at six. But that is not necessarily jumping the queue, butting in line. It's one human to another. It's how we say thank you. It's how they shake hands. But the jumping the queue thing? No.*

Another philanthropist underlined the difficult value judgments that are embroiled in the discussion.

> *Would I expect preferential treatment? Yes and no. Yes in the sense that if I funded you and have a relationship with you, it would be just like if your neighbor was a great cardiac surgeon or something. If someone in my family had a spinal cord injury, I'd expect to call up for the guy and ask him advice and ask, "What would you do?" That's the yes part. I don't expect to jump to the head of the line because I made a donation. I don't think it should work that way. I'm not naive; I know that happens.*

Even after that experience, he doesn't see this as a black-and-white issue. As one whose philanthropic giving is focused on health care, he senses the vagaries.

> *I mean, it's human nature to have priorities, and it's foolish to think that there isn't favouritism going on of some kind. I personally don't agree necessarily that you should be able to buy whatever you want, but I know it happens in some cases.*

Charles Juravinski

- Founder and former owner of Flamboro Downs racetrack
- Benefactor of the Juravinski Hospital and Juravinski Cancer Centre in Hamilton, Ontario
- Supporter of numerous other health-related and communal causes

Full bio on page 132

Charles Juravinski's views move the discussion to the opposite end of the spectrum. Even after giving more than $53 million to health care institutions, he remarkably told us, "I can answer that without equivocation. I wait in line the same as everybody else. I insist on it." Illustrating that this wasn't just bluster, he told us about an occasion when he needed treatment for a medical condition. "I make a telephone call to my vascular surgeon the same as everyone else. I get an ultrasound the same as anyone else, and I get in line to get my operation the same as everyone else, end of story."

Tony Comper

- Immediate past president and CEO of BMO Financial Group
- Founder (along with his late wife, Elizabeth) and principal supporter of FAST—Fighting Antisemitism Together
- Director of many corporations and philanthropic organizations

Full bio, see page 125

Tony Comper echoed those sentiments. When asked whether philanthropists should receive preferential treatment, his response left no room for interpretation.

That's a conflict of interest. I just find it's unseemly. Let me put it that way—to think that there's kind of a quid pro quo. I pay for my own opera tickets.

Whether as a by-product of relationships, out of a sense of obligation, or simply as a way of saying thank you, offering a donor perks makes her feel like an insider. And that can only increase her sense of affinity to an organization and ultimately the likelihood of continuing her support.

We acknowledge that this is a very thorny ethical issue. There are those who feel that providing a donor with any form of preferred treatment is immoral. At one of our early presentations on this subject, we were confronted by a seasoned fundraiser who was deeply offended by the topic.

The challenge for the fundraiser is to find the perk, if any, that is right for each donor while maintaining the integrity of the organization. On this issue, we are not advocates for any particular approach. We can only report that done well, it has the potential to deepen relationships with the philanthropists.

True Givers Are Not Selfless

Perks may be controversial, as we would like to believe that givers are truly selfless individuals. As it happens, reality suggests the contrary. One research study analyzed the selflessness levels of Canada's most generous and community-focused individuals—the recipients of the Caring Canadian Award. Paradoxically, when these Caring Canadians were compared to those with no history of volunteerism or communal involvement, the Caring Canadians actually scored higher on self-interest than their counterparts.[14]

Some may find these results disheartening, but studies suggest that pure selflessness, termed pathological altruism, is actually proved to be unhealthy and unsustainable. The research suggests that those who focused on everyone else's needs, to the exclusion of their own, not only harmed themselves but proved unable to sustain their giving over the long term.[15]

8

*It is one of the beautiful compensations of this life that no one can
sincerely try to help another without helping himself.*

—Ralph Waldo Emerson

Appeal to the Philanthropist and the Businessperson

When the prospect of business results is added to philanthropic intent, a powerful combination is created. Harnessing that power is often the key to the success of a fundraising campaign or initiative.

When asked about the most creative fundraising solicitation he had ever received, Issy Sharp pointed to a proposal made in support of a new opera house for Toronto. What made this so noteworthy? It appealed to Sharp's business interests. Wisely, the fundraising team offered corporate naming rights in perpetuity. It would be the Four Seasons Centre for the Performing Arts forever. That got Sharp's attention and, in his words, here's why.

> *Because of the way opera is considered worldwide, it's very high end, internationally well respected. If we could get our company on [the opera house] in perpetuity, that would be a good investment in terms of marketing.*

Sharp immediately saw the alignment between his company, Four Seasons Hotels, as a high-end luxury brand and the upscale audience generally attracted to the opera. The result was a $20 million donation.

From his reflections, it's apparent that Sharp was able to see the many facets of the corporate contribution.

[It was] a good cause, but also it was self-serving. You know, it was a quid pro quo. I saw that this [contribution] could do so much because so many people were going to benefit. The government was behind it. [The corporate contribution] was going to bring a lot of money to the table from private enterprise, and it was going to do something for the city, giving it one of the best opera houses in the world. And from a company point of view, our name is up there forever. So that was something that we could afford, and I just simply looked at it and said, "How much money do we spend on marketing and advertising?" This was a small piece. We [amortized] it over five years, and it became an easy way to justify a cost that I looked at as a marketing tool.

For the Canadian Opera Company, this was the philanthropic kick start they were looking for, but for Sharp, this was a shrewd marketing initiative. As he puts it, "So it had a lot of good things. That's what a good business deal is. Both parties feel they are getting value."

But the story doesn't end there. It gets better. Once Sharp's interests were tied to the fortunes of the opera house, the fundraisers made another prudent move. On the strength of his corporate support, they sought a personal contribution. This is Sharp's account of that request.

To finish the campaign because they were still short, they said, "Look, we appreciate [what you've done], and you can just say no. Nobody is going to object. You had your company donate, but what about you personally?"

That resulted in a $5 million donation from Issy and his wife Rosalie. In the end, Sharp sees only the benefit of their personal philanthropy.

We personally made a major contribution, and that brought the rest of the board on side to finish [the campaign] and raise [the funds], and there was no debt.

In the final analysis, a clever appeal to Sharp's business interests resulted in $25 million in funding directly related to him and his company, not to mention the additional support it helped to secure.

Gerald Sheff has an amazing story that speaks to the intersection of business and philanthropic interests.

In 1994, the Art Gallery of Ontario (AGO) was making plans to bring the Barnes

Foundation Exhibition, a prestigious selection of works by Renoir, Cézanne, Van Gogh, Picasso, and Monet, to Toronto. Fundraisers were seeking $300,000 in sponsorship support from each of three companies, totaling the $900,000 required to fund the exhibit. Gluskin Sheff, the investment firm that Gerald cofounded, was one of those three.

It didn't take long for Sheff and his partner, Ira Gluskin, to see a unique opportunity to align their business interest with the AGO's philanthropic needs.

> *Now, we had been in business ten years, and our tenth anniversary was coming up. We had a blockbuster year in our tenth year. We had shot the lights out, really done very, very well. I talked to Ira [Gluskin] and said, "I think we have an opportunity here, but we don't want to be partners [with the two other companies]. We want to own this ourselves. If we're going to do this, this is Gluskin Sheff. We have the opportunity to buy this thing, and I think it can be very, very big. It is right in our sweet spot because it's culture, it's prestige. It's the Art Gallery of Ontario. It appeals to wealthy people. It relates to our clientele. It is everything that is upscale and nothing that is downscale."*

In considering their emerging proposal to be the sole sponsor, Gluskin and Sheff reasoned that the AGO was going to be spared the time and resource of courting two other prospective sponsors. This led to Sheff's conclusion. "I said I know we can buy this for less [than] nine hundred [thousand], maybe seven hundred. We could get a deal if we bought the whole thing." So they made their pitch to the AGO and said, "We could be interested, but we want the whole thing exclusively. We want to be the sponsor of the Barnes. We want to own it, and we want it branded as Gluskin Sheff, the sponsor of the Barnes. So how much do you want for it?"

The final negotiated single sponsorship amount was $750,000. But there was an unforeseen glitch.

> *We naively did not realize that the first thing the press would want to know was how much we [Gluskin Sheff] paid. We thought that information was going to be private. That was very naive on our part because the only thing that really mattered to them was how much money they got for this property. So once we realized the number was going to be public, we ourselves stepped up and said that we can't go with $750 [thousand]. It has to be a million. We've got to have that $1 million sponsorship because at the time we were a company that had a million-dollar minimum for investors. $750 [thousand] sounds like it is a discount operation. We've got to set a bar here. It's got to be*

a million dollars.

Let's take a moment to recap. The AGO correctly anticipated that there was a potential convergence of business and philanthropic interests related to the Barnes exhibit. However, what could not possibly be anticipated was that the total sponsorship would ultimately be $1 million. This was a result of the uniquely symbiotic relationship between Gluskin Sheff's business interests and the AGO's philanthropic needs. What was the true end result? Here are Sheff's interesting comments.

> *Basically, the sponsorship was a million dollars. Now again, was that charity or was that business? You tell me. For us, it was business; for them, it was charity. Was that philanthropy? I don't know.*

Sheff and Gluskin didn't stop there. They sought to capitalize on the benefit that would accrue from being the sponsor of the Barnes, and the AGO was a collateral beneficiary. This is Sheff's account.

> *The AGO has never had a success in its history like they had with the Barnes because we took that million-dollar sponsorship and said, "Okay, nobody sees [the exhibit] until our guests see it." We threw the opening party for the Barnes. The party cost us an additional $1 million, but the party was front-page news … It was incredible for business because everybody came.*

He went on to describe how an invitation to the party became a hot ticket and an opportunity to hobnob with Canada's elite. It was exactly what they wanted.

Sheff's final analysis again speaks to how a philanthropic need can be fulfilled through satisfying business interests.

> *It was a phenomenal $2 million that we spent because it put us on the map ten years into business in a way that we could never have done. Is that philanthropy? That's advertising.*

Gary Slaight

- President and CEO, Slaight Communications, and former owner of Standard Broadcasting
- Through the Slaight Family Foundation, major supporter of many of Toronto's hospitals
- Supporter of numerous arts-based organizations, as well as global relief, educational, and communal causes

Full bio on page 139

Corporate philanthropy and social responsibility are accepted and even expected practice in today's business world. That wasn't the case in 1985 when the Slaight family bought Standard Broadcasting. Their commitment to use their radio stations to fulfill a philanthropic end was trailblazing and, according to Gary Slaight, turned into the philanthropic project of which he is most proud.

> When we bought Standard from Conrad Black in '85, they had done their
> first fundraiser for SickKids [Hospital], and they had raised like $1,000 or
> something. We just decided to keep doing it, so it just grew. And when we sold
> [Standard] four years ago, I think we raised $4 million in two days. We
> turned over all our radio stations in Toronto and did an on-air [radiothon].
> We interviewed kids and doctors and broadcast from the hospital.

In the course of twenty-two years, the Standard radiothons raised over $25 million for the Hospital for Sick Children, resulting in the dedication of the Slaight Family Atrium. The institution certainly benefited. As Gary explains, so did the company.

> It was a great thing to do, but it also had benefits for us coming back because
> of the goodwill in the community and the good feelings it gave the employees,
> the good feelings it gave our clients. You know all the clients on the radio
> stations were proud of us.

Even as he was selling the company, Gary found ways to bring his philanthropic and business interests together.

> The best thing we did was when we sold the company to Astral Media—
> which was about three years ago. Part of the deal was that I get a large
> amount of inventory [of airtime] to use for public service announcements for
> charities I'm working with. So I give it out. I use it for Free the Children, Kids
> Help Phone, anybody that I'm trying to help out, and that's for ten years.

In a similar vein, Larry Rosen described a philanthropic initiative of Harry Rosen, the men's clothing retailer of which he is the CEO.

> We did a little bit of research, and we found that there is a tremendous
> alignment between cancer research and what our customers wanted us to do
> from a charitable point of view and what our associates wanted us to do. So
> we decided on cancer research as an important cause. Then we started
> thinking about it a little more. We saw that prostate cancer, which affects one
> in six men, is the most common cancer, and is the largest killer of men (believe
> it or not), was not being taken serious in research. So we started making that
> our cause, and eventually, it evolved. We ultimately developed two races—one
> in Toronto, one in Vancouver called Harry's Spring Run-off. Between the two,

it raises a half-million dollars a year for prostate cancer research.

Recognizing that their target demographic was predominantly male, they wisely chose a philanthropic initiative that would resonate with customers. And it has produced impressive results. In five years, the program has raised over $2.5 million in support of prostate cancer research. Admirably, Larry is integrally involved in the allocation of the funds so that he can say, "We make sure every penny that we raise goes right to [research]."

Larry Rosen

- Chairman and CEO of Harry Rosen
- Board member, Princess Margaret Hospital Foundation, and member of the Ivey School of Business advisory board
- Major supporter of many cancer research initiatives
- Supporter of numerous educational, communal, and health-related causes

For full bio, see page 137

As is often the case when philanthropists use their business interest to fulfill charitable goals, there are many winners. Here's how Larry describes that.

So at the end of the day, our clients appreciate the fact that we are an organization that gives and that believes in giving, and there are so many wins involved. I mean, is it good for our company that our customers are aware that we are seriously committed to giving and making a difference in the community? Absolutely. It's a very positive thing. I mean, people like to deal with people who give, right? It is a huge win with our customers; our [sales] associates feel very fulfilled. They feel a great sense of pride that we are making a difference.

Brett Wilson was even more candid about the intersection of charitable giving and corporate positioning.

Every time [FirstEnergy] gave a contribution to a charity, we were very open about the fact that we expected something in return. What we gained in the form of public recognition, cobranding with larger companies, or recognition with the charity's network helped us to dramatically increase our profile, develop new partnerships, and grow our client base.

Wilson's post-gift strategy was brilliant and should be a guide to any business owner wanting to leverage his philanthropy.

When we first started making donations to charities, I would make a point of sending the cheque—signed by myself and when possible another senior partner of the firm—directly to the CEO or executive director of the charity, with a copy going to the second in command. We would also send a copy of each cheque to selected board members, clients, potential clients, and competitors and their spouses who were known supporters of that charity. Instead of lumping ourselves with a list of donors captured on the back page of the charity's annual report, which would probably not get noticed, we made a point, at cost of a letter or two, of building our brand with thousands of people who had the potential to help with goodwill for FirstEnergy.

Leslie Dan

- Founder, Novopharm, now Teva Canada
- Member, Order of Canada and Order of Ontario
- Founder CAN-MAP, an organization that provides medicine to developing countries
- Supporter of numerous medical causes

For full bio, see page 127

We give the last word on the intersection of business and philanthropic interests to Leslie Dan. When asked about the philanthropic activity or gift of which he is most proud, he told us this.

In 1985, I started an organization called CAN-MAP—the Canadian Medicine Aid Programme. Every year, we donate large amounts of medicine to sick people in the third world, which is delivered by medical doctors, charitable organizations, nurses. Last year, we gave about $4-5 million worth of medicine, and this year, it will be the same amount.

Most tellingly, when asked whether this was a corporate philanthropic program, he responded, "Well, that is part of me."

For many philanthropists, business interests are a highly effective means of fulfilling charitable goals. The fact that corporate benefits might accrue doesn't diminish the very personal motivation at the root of the activity. The accomplished fundraiser will understand that once the philanthropist is motivated to give, business concerns may be the key to maximizing the gift.

Doing Well by Doing Good

"Those who give more, earn more" isn't just a pleasant-sounding platitude. Recent research has supported this notion with empirical data.[16] With data aggregated from nearly thirty thousand Americans, economist Arthur Brooks has demonstrated that for every additional $1 of charitable giving, individuals' future incomes increased by $3.75.

These findings were also confirmed by the research of professors Baruch Lev and Christine Petrovits of New York University's Stern School of Business and Suresh Radhakrishnan of the University of Texas at Dallas's Naveen Jindal School of Management. They concluded that doing good leads to doing well, as greater corporate charitable gifts were highly correlated with enhanced future revenues.[17] Several mutual funds were even formed on the premise that companies who concern themselves with the health of their communities will be rewarded with superior returns, investing exclusively in companies known for charitable giving.[18]

9

There is a saying that every nice piece of work needs the right person in the right place at the right time.

—Benoit Mandelbrot

It's All About the Right Person

I f the three keys to real estate success are location, location, and location, then the keys to fundraising success are people, people, and people. Don't even bother trying to get around that. In fundraising, as in business, the perfect pitch starts with the perfect person.

David Kassie tells an illuminating story about being solicited for a gift.

> *I got approached by two prominent members of the community. And they said, "We'd like you to give X amount." And I said, "Okay." And they said, "Really?" And I said, "Sure." I said, "Why wouldn't I give to the community?" They were like, "You're kidding!" And I said, "Thank you so much for taking the time and coming to see people like me. That's very, very nice of you."*

Clearly, he was honoured that these two prominent individuals would take the time to see him. What's revealing is that he took the meeting without knowing what it was about. "I didn't even know why they were there, actually. I had like a hundred meetings a day at that point, so it was on my calendar marked in with their names."

So it was the right names that got the appointment, and clearly, it was the right people who were able to get the gift. As Kassie says, "Having two people who I didn't know well but I knew of and who were so prominent was much more compelling ..."

David Cynamon

• Executive Chairman, K2 Pure Solutions, and founder, KIK Custom Products
• Former owner of the Toronto Argonauts
• Benefactor of the David and Stacey Cynamon Chair in Critical Care Medicine at Toronto's SickKids Hospital, as well as a supporter of many health and communal causes

For full bio, see page 126

Sometime it's not just the name but also the reputation of the person who is asking that can lead to success. David Cynamon had decided he wanted to support Mount Sinai Hospital. To make the deal, he arranged an appointment with Lawrence Bloomberg, who was chair of the hospital's foundation. This, according to Cynamon, is how it played out.

I went to them. They didn't solicit me. I went into Lawrence Bloomberg's office. I felt that Sinai was important, Jewish hospital, all those things. So what I planned to give ended up being two and half times [larger] because Lawrence Bloomberg is as good as it gets.

Interesting situation. The donor took the initiative to contact the organization with a view to making a gift. He's even decided how much he wanted to give. But then the fundraiser essentially says, "Thank you very much, but that's not enough. Here's what I say you are going to give." How did Bloomberg manage this fundraising feat? Cynamon provides some detail.

I came in, and I told him, "This is what I'd like to give," and basically he told me what I am going to give. It was then up to me to say, "No, Lawrence, screw you," or "Yeah, you're right, Lawrence, I should be giving that."

And what was David's reaction to what some regard as real chutzpah?

As a guiding light and a guy I trust and a mentor and a friend of my late father-in-law, it didn't bother me. And again, remember, it was one of my early North American [major donations], so for all I knew, I was giving too little, and here is Lawrence Bloomberg, the most experienced guy. If he says that's how much I should be giving, who am I to argue? But only Lawrence could get away with that.

Cynamon wasn't offended. He acceded to Bloomberg's will. Give credit to Bloomberg for recognizing the uniqueness of the situation and capitalizing on it.

Even years later, reflecting on that particular gift, Cynamon has no misgivings. "It is what it is, and I didn't mind."

That meeting and the gift that ensued lent real-life credence to Gerald Sheff's analysis of the role that the right person can play.

> *Who is asking trumps even what they are asking for. That is just the way it is. Often there is an imbalance between the power relation between who is being asked and who is asking. Who is asking is more important than what they are asking for.*

Issy Sharp's experience has brought him to a similar conclusion.

> *It all depends on the person. If they say, "Look, we need X dollars," you normally might not give it if it was somebody else asking. But that person comes with a little more influence. It's the person who asks who is probably the strongest means of raising money.*

Many of our interviewees disagreed on the question of whether it's best to meet with a staff person or a layperson when a gift is being solicited. However, they all understood that having the right person present could make or break the opportunity. They just disagreed on who that person should be. Here are good representations of the opposing points of view.

In one corner, we have Kelly Meighen.

> *I would think most donors want to hear from the guy or the woman who is ultimately going to carry the ball—if that's the president of the university or a dean, or the CEO of the hospital or the researcher. Because, you know, it's an old adage, but it's true that people don't give to institutions, they give to other people.*

And from the other corner, here is Issy Sharp.

> *You're never going to give money to the professional. You're going to give information, but it's the individual who is coming to talk, and if he is personally going to be part of it, you will listen. It's easy to say no to a professional because there is no connection. It is much more difficult to say no to a personal friend who is already going to do what he is asking you to do.*

What might make the meeting even more successful is if that friend is a fellow philanthropist. Based on this strong personal observation from Fred Waks, a philanthropist-to-philanthropist pitch would be ideal.

> *So it's important to me in terms of my friendships, my business life, and my family life in particular that I like to be with people in the philanthropy*

business. If somebody's a philanthropist, I will go the extra mile to do something for them; if they're not, I will go the extra mile to make sure they're not part of my life. So it's really that black and white. Tie always goes to the philanthropist."

Larry Kinlin

- President, Larry Kinlin & Associates Inc.
- Benefactor of the Larry Kinlin School of Business at Fanshawe College in London, Ontario
- Board member, SickKids Hospital Foundation and other charitable organizations

For full bio, see page 133

Just how much can the right person contribute to the success of a solicitation? Larry Kinlin provided this almost unbelievable story about his efforts on behalf of United Way that emphatically answers that question. It also offers an interesting perspective on staff and laypeople at the solicitation. Please note that to protect the identity of the philanthropists in his stories, Larry used alternate names.

I knew where there was a million-dollar gift, and I knew the person. He happened to be a client of mine, which was an unfair advantage, but everybody knew that this person had means. So I said to the executive director and CEO of the organization, "We just need to go see John, and we're going to ask him for a million dollars."

So I called John, and I said, "John, we'd like to talk to you." John said, "About what, Larry?" I said, "Money, John. Money. That's what we want to talk about." John said, "Well, as always, Larry, you're pretty clear." So we picked a morning and went to his beautiful home. The executive director was very nervous. So we walked in and sat down. And he always was super direct in everything.

John said, "So, Larry, what's on your mind?" I said, "Well, do you want it short or long?" He said, "Oh, short, short." I said, "I want a million dollars. That's it. We'll put your name on the building, but we want a million dollars." When we came in, we did briefly talk about how this would be a great campaign for the city, et cetera, but it was a three-minute dialogue because this guy's so sharp they make razor blades out of him.

This all happened within seven to eight minutes. He said, "I'll give you six hundred thousand bucks." I said, "John, that's not good enough." "What do you mean it's not good enough?" he replied. I said, "There's a rule. If you want to put your name up there on that building, it's a million dollars. Otherwise,

> we'll have to go find somebody else. And I love you, John, but that's the way it's going to be." John said, "You're serious?" I answered, "Certainly, I'm serious. It's there forever. It's a great gift that you can give to this community. So $600,000, $700,000, do I hear $1 million?" The executive director was really having a tough time with this because he doesn't ever get involved with that kind of banter.
>
> I knew it was there. He goes, "Okay, okay, let's do it. Talk to my lawyer. He'll get this all worked out."
>
> And that was it. It was a million dollars. It took eight minutes of our time. But I was ready to be ready. I knew what we were doing, and I knew why. And he knew that I was coming for a reason, and he really wanted to give something back.

There are occasions when having the right people involved will cement the philanthropist's involvement as opposed to the gift. Representatives of LOFT Community Services wanted James Fleck to be the honouree at an upcoming fundraising dinner, and he was resisting. Fleck picks up the story.

> People were after me to have this dinner, and I was kind of fighting it off. And then they finally came to me and said, "We've got Roger Martin, Karen Kain, Red Wilson, and Albert Schultz as the four co-chairs." And I said, "With a group like that, I'd come to this dinner." So I said yes, and we went ahead with it.

David Cynamon's extensive philanthropic experience has brought him to an understanding of how the right person can make a difference that some might consider cynical.

> Causes are very smart. They have a chairman, a co-chairman, executive chairman. They got a chairman for everything: chairman for the bathroom, the toilet, the sink, everything. Because inevitably there's a name on there that you owe something to. And inevitably it comes down to the name.

The truth is that he's right. It's the right name—the right person—that can motivate a decision. Having as many names as possible increases the chances that a prospective donor is going to fund someone he or she considers influential.

We conclude the discussion with Brendan Calder, who nicely sums up the dynamic and adds an interesting distinction between time and money.

I don't give money to causes. Yeah, I don't. I give to people that I know will do something useful with this money. I can't remember ever giving to a cause. I give time to a cause. I give money to people.

10

A decision is made with the brain. A commitment is made with the heart. Therefore, a commitment is much deeper and more binding than a decision.

—Nido Qubein

Passion is the Prerequisite

Fundraisers, like businesspeople, are always searching for the key ingredient that will make a pitch successful. Based on our interviews, we can tell you that the secret sauce in the recipe for a successful solicitation is, unquestionably, passion.

David Cynamon established the need for passion as a general principle when he talked about what distinguished the best solicitations that have been made to him.

> *I think first and foremost, like any business, it is the presenter. How passionate is that presenter, how much energy is in that presenter. Really, a good presenter could probably sell you anything and get you to donate to anything.*

Martin Connell dug deeper into what embodies the passion and energy to which Cynamon referred and defines the attributes of a great fundraiser.

> *I think there are a handful of people in this city who run institutions who are truly charismatic. They have an incredible capacity to intrigue and inspire the listener to want to be engaged. If you're going to be in the fundraising business you better have a charismatic person sitting across the table who can spin the story in a way that captures your attention.*

It's interesting that Connell went on to associate those qualities with seniority.

> *It depends, I guess, on the seniority of the person. I mean, I don't want to sit across from a junior fundraising officer. I know full off that that person doesn't necessarily carry the same passion, so I want to be motivated.*

In summary, he presented a précis of the successful solicitor that could apply to any industry or sector.

> *They all drink from the same thing, same fountain, great passion, and great belief in what they do and a great ability to sell.*

So we've established that philanthropists think that passion is an essential characteristic of the great persuader. But is there any evidence that it really works? Don Johnson provided an account that emphatically answers that question.

> *In terms of where I have responded to a solicitation, I guess the most creative [solicitation] would have been from the United Way, when Frances Lankin, the CEO of United Way, came to see me with Tony Bell, who was chairing the campaign. She articulated a great vision for this concept of community hubs.*

Hearing this, we probed a little deeper. Was it just a matter of creativity that made this meeting so successful? Johnson's answer was revealing.

> *It wasn't just the creativity. She really had a tremendous vision and passion to have United Way help the people in Toronto, particularly in disadvantaged neighborhoods in a really meaningful way. It was not just the creativity.*

Establishing just how successful Lankin and her passion were, Johnson made this incredible confession. "I had no intention of making a million-dollar donation, but [because of her passion] I did."

If that wasn't good enough, listen to what happened after he made the commitment.

> *As a matter of fact, what happened is that she got some additional support. It was about a million [dollars] for a catalyst to get everything together for this community hub, and she managed to get additional funding from other sources, so they only needed $700,000 of my donation to build the hub. So there was $300,000 left over, and she convinced me to dedicate it to another community hub in the west end. That was matched by three other organizations, which financed another hub.*

Mark Krembil

- Former co-owner of retail company Lewiscraft
- Board member of biotech firms and many nonprofit organizations
- Benefactor of the Krembil Centre for Stem Cell Biology at Robarts Research Institute in London, Ontario, and Krembil Chair in Neuroscience at Toronto Western Hospital
- Supporter of numerous health research and children's causes

For full bio, see page 134

Lankin's success in securing an additional $300,000 in government funding should have let Johnson off the hook for that amount. However, her passion convinced Johnson to keep his money in the game, allowing it to be parlayed into even more support for related projects.

Based on what Mark Krembil had to say, passion can even turn a no into a yes. He started by telling us about the no.

So we funded some work at a hospital, and at the end of that, they came back with another proposal, and it was five times larger in scope to the one we originally did. So that kind of scared me a little bit. Then looking at it, it was way over my head, very esoteric. And so that was a no. I wasn't going to fund that grant.

That sounded pretty resolute, but it changed.

We reconnected, and later on, I spent more time with the scientist. I guess I kind of adopted their passion for what they're doing and the novel nature. And so basically, I changed my mind.

How did Krembil account for the change of heart? "The reason it went from no to a yes is primarily because of interaction with the scientist." Putting his previous terms of reference into the formula, it was the scientist's passion that won him over.

Mark wraps up the story with a powerful observation. Although he frames it in very personal terms, fundraisers should pay attention to his message about how passion can be completely compelling.

If you have a lot of passion in something, I'll have time for you. I'll want to know why you have [that passion]. I'm a curious mind. So if you believe it so strongly I'll give you a chance. I'll give myself a chance to see if I can believe you.

Here's an example from Naomi Azrieli of how passion can make an indelible mark.

I had this most unbelievable experience in Houston, of all places, where I was checking out an institute that does work on neurological disorders. I was talking to the woman who not only ran it but thought the whole thing up. It was her baby from beginning to end. And I had never spoken to someone with so much passion and so much dedication. And I thought, I have no idea if we're going to work with her. We may end up making other decisions, but I thought that this is someone you want to partner with because she so clearly believed in what she was doing, and she was so knowledgeable.

Our definition of passion is being augmented as we go. Energy, charisma, experience, vision, and based on Azrieli's account, knowledge and a sense of proprietorship are all important. Naomi added one more: love.

And there are a number of people that I've met who are really passionate about what they do. I think you have to be passionate about what you do. You have to love what you do.

There's a business adage that says, "Sales is a transfer of emotion." To get someone to buy something, you have to make them feel something. Philanthropic transactions are no different. Passion is the most effective demonstration of emotion.

Issy Sharp's account of how he came to support Terry Fox in the early days of his cross-Canada run for cancer research is truly inspirational. It demonstrates how the passion of one individual can capture a philanthropist's imagination and lead to that passion being conveyed exponentially to others.

I was one of the original supporters of what he was doing—running across Canada. I'd give him a good meal, a good night's sleep. But then he ran up against a brick wall. And I had somebody who was just tracking him, and she was saying, "It's terrible. Nobody believes in him. They are almost making fun of him." Because it was a ridiculous thing for him to say he was going to run across Canada. Everyone thought it was a gimmick. What's this kid up to? Nobody believed that this was his real intent. They thought that it was a publicity gag. So I decided that as a company we would make a contribution. I think it was $2 for every mile or kilometer, and that would come to $10,000, and I took out ads in the magazines and newspapers and challenged 999 other companies to join forces, and that would make it a $10 million run. And I told him, I got the word to him that this is what we were going to do. Well, he heard about that, and he called me from a pay telephone on the highway and was crying over the telephone. You know, this was a young kid, seventeen or eighteen years old, and he said, you know, he was just ready to quit. He was so dejected, so

> *depressed, and he said that if one person cares enough to do what you've done, he said, "That's all I need. And I'm going to keep going until I can't."*

We can see the powerfully cyclical nature of passion. The person whose passion is the catalyst to philanthropic giving is, in turn, inspired by the passion of those who gave. But it was Sharp's indelible passion that takes this story to today—and beyond.

> *He ran his heart out, he had to stop, cancer took over, and I arranged with he and his family that we would hold a run each year in his honour. But he didn't want anybody to finish it. He didn't want it to be a competition, like he was, running to help other people. So that's what we did, and we just celebrated our thirtieth year, and we've raised over $500 million for cancer research.*

Eric Sprott's thoughts shed light on the inverse of what we're discussing. What happens when the philanthropist feels no passion?

> *The ones that aggravate me the most are when the donation request is sorrow based. Like this is such a desperate situation, there's no hope ... and I think to myself, Then why would I give to something where there is no hope? That's not inspiring me to give. So you're basically telling me that this is such a terrible situation that it's not ever going to get any better? That's what it feels like. Why would I give to something where there is no chance of things improving?*

Philip Reichmann

- Co-founder, ReichmannHauer Capital Partners, a real estate development firm
- Board member of Mount Sinai Hospital, Friends of Simon Wiesenthal Center for Holocaust Studies, and may other organizations
- Supporter of numerous educational and communal causes

For full bio, see page 136

There is no shortage of problems, causes, or issues being brought to the attention of philanthropists. The key is to stand out. Passion invokes a sense of purpose—the feeling that the philanthropist's money is going to make a difference.

To this point, we've been discussing the impact of passion on securing the financial commitment. If passion will get someone to part with his or her money, will it do the same for his or her time? According to Philip Reichmann, the answer to that would be yes. The specific question we asked him was this: "What distinguishes the organizations you're willing to roll up your sleeves and fundraise for and those that you aren't?" This was his answer.

> *Different things, but I have to feel passionate about it. I have to feel committed to it. I won't fundraise for something that I don't care about. I*

can't. You have to believe in what you're selling. Whatever it is—whether it is a product or a service or a charity.

It's very clear that passion is the prerequisite for success in motivating the philanthropist to action. Passion was also at the core of much of the advice offered by our interviewees to budding philanthropists. Here is Gil Palter's counsel:

It's the same advice I give young people with regard to their careers, which is find something that you actually like, that you're passionate about, that you care about, and just get involved. Find an area that actually resonates with you. Because going through the motions never results in a great outcome. Doing something because you love it almost always results in a great outcome.

Linda Frum's advice was from the heart. Inasmuch as it was offered to those just getting started in philanthropy, it could serve as an effective rallying call to anyone involved in any nonprofit or social enterprise. And it's a fitting message with which to close the chapter on passion.

So my advice would be to be fearless about [philanthropy] and to be passionate. If you see a problem or an issue or cause that needs attention, it's okay to try and harness other people's energy towards that project. It's not just okay, it's good, and you should do it fearlessly and passionately.

Joy and Passion Versus Duty and Obligation

What's the impact of passion being central to our giving? Psychologists Netta Weinstein and Richard Ryan demonstrate that giving has an energizing effect on us—providing givers with a sense of fulfillment and empowerment—only when done with passion and joy.[19]

Conversely, when giving was done out of duty or obligation, it had no positive impact on our energy levels or well-being.

ⅠⅠ

Money and time are the heaviest burdens of life,
and the unhappiest of all mortals are those who have more
of either than they know how to use.

—Samuel Johnson

The Involvement Paradox

Our interviews corroborated what fundraisers have known for years—charitable gifts most often emerge from a philanthropist's involvement with an organization. To get more gifts, you need to get more givers actively involved with your cause. But here's the rub. For most of our interviewees, time is more precious than money.

In truth, there is a cyclical relationship between involvement and giving that Kelly Meighen astutely explained.

> *It's like the chicken-and-the-egg thing. You get involved in something. You are drawn to an organization for a myriad of reasons. Then the involvement facilitates a gift, or a gift precipitates further involvement. And I think particularly when you're making what we consider to be a significant financial commitment, you make it because you're involved. You make it because you understand the organization.*

The quantum of charitable support that can emanate from involvement can be impressive. Donald Johnson's $5 million contribution to the eye centre at Toronto Western Hospital came after almost twenty years of involvement with the organization. Here's his account of the journey that led to his momentous gift:

> *I was invited on to a board of an organization called the Eye Research Institute of Canada. I was interested because of my problems with glaucoma, and I agreed to chair a fundraising campaign in the late '80s. I did not know much about fundraising then, and to make a long story short, I ended up going on the board of the institute and then took over as chair. An opportunity arose to attract a real star, one of the top researchers in eye disease in the United States. I said we should offer him the position here, but the hospital and the university couldn't put together sufficient funding to offer him the kind of compensation, research support, and facilities he needed to make the move. That triggered my decision. If the hospital and university cannot do it, someone had to do it. I decided after a few weeks to make the $5 million pledge to what is now, for some reason, called the Donald K. Johnson Eye Centre.*

Hal Jackman's experiences at the opera house and the University of Toronto mirror Johnson's experience.

> *I was interested in the opera, but I think I got on the board before I gave money. The same with the University of Toronto, which are the two things I have given most to. I was involved in the university before I really made the decision to give money to them.*

If you're wondering to what degree involvement can pay off, consider that Jackman's support for U of T exceeded $30 million. Jackman also introduced an interesting nuance to the discussion. To this point, it would almost seem that charitable support was just a natural outgrowth of involvement. However, it could be that involvement, particularly at leadership levels, imposes a kind of moral imperative to give. This is Jackman's view:

> *I think if they decide to make you president or chancellor, perhaps there is an expectation, if you are financially capable of making a donation, that you will. And that influences you.*

For Larry Rosen, taking a decision-making role doesn't just create expectations of financial support. Rather, he sees it as an obligation.

> *Part of the thing about being on a board is you have to have the time, the belief in the cause, and you have to be prepared to open your wallet to the cause. If the board members don't step up with major gifts and major support of the institution, who else is going to do so?*

Gerry Schwartz

- Chief executive officer, Onex Corporation
- Director of many Canadian corporations
- Benefactor of Gerald Schwartz School of Business at St. Francis Xavier University
- With his wife, Heather Reisman, major supporter of Toronto's Mount Sinai Hospital and many other communal causes
- Officer, Order of Canada

For full bio, see page 137

Sometimes greater involvement allows a philanthropist to exceed his or her own giving expectations. When we asked Gerry Schwartz what accounted for situations in which he gave more money to a cause than he had originally anticipated, he responded, "More involvement, more liking it, more understanding it, more seeing it succeed, more wanting it to succeed, more wanting to finance it succeeding." He backed that up with a case in point from his own experience.

> *I will give you an example—Eva's Phoenix, which is a housing project that is part of Eva's Initiatives. My friend Buzz Hargrove introduced me to the organization. I went and saw it with him, was unbelievably impressed, made an initial commitment to it. That commitment was $100,000 a year for three years. At the end of three years, Buzz asked me to get reinvigorated in it. I went and saw what they had [done] up to that date. I think they've done a fantastic job. I think they made fantastically good use of the money. I think they're well governed, well run, and successful. And so it became more and more interesting to continue to make larger commitments to them.*

For many, involvement is an important part of their philanthropy. James Fleck explains.

> *My philanthropy is usually action oriented. I'm usually involved in whatever it is. So like with the Power Plant [art gallery at Harbourfront in Toronto], I was the chairman. I got the board, hired the first director. So it's not just on the money side.*

Fleck, however, has no illusions about it. Time is not offered to the exclusion of money. It's more a matter of sequence.

> *Well, usually what happens is that I want to get my hands involved, and then the money follows. It's unusual that the money goes and then I want to get involved.*

Larry Tanenbaum

- Chair, Maple Leaf Sports & Entertainment, chair and CEO, Kilmer Van Nostrand Co., Ltd.
- Benefactor of the Lunenfeld-Tanenbaum Research Institute at Toronto's Mount Sinai Hospital
- Officer, Order of Canada
- Supporter of numerous educational, health-related, and communal causes

For full bio, see page 142

Larry Tanenbaum feels that the value of time and energy that one offers a cause is often greater than even very generous financial support. In his view, philanthropy is most powerful when time and money go hand in hand.

Anybody can get lucky in business, can make some money. A lot of people just give money away to write a cheque and be gone. But actually involving yourself in causes and building around any type of giving is something that you're giving to them apart from money— along with money. So you're giving something —whether that's your thoughts or some ideas about building the organization.

Tanenbaum's commitment to those principles has led him to be an active practitioner of catalytic philanthropy—a term coined by Mark Kramer, a corporate social responsibility innovator and Harvard fellow.[15] It describes transformative modes that philanthropists can use to provide their support. Larry sees this as the optimal way in which he can help.

I can really make a difference with what I do. I am really directing my attention to a number of projects where the money, the time I spend can truly transform a part of an organization—an idea into something more.

Not only is this the way that he chooses to engage, Tanenbaum also sees this synergistic type of involvement as a compelling means of soliciting the philanthropist's support.

So the cause resonates, but the people who are asking you are incredibly involved. They are not just looking for the money. They want you to be involved in the ideas and share their vision for what the institution can be.

To this point, we have reaffirmed the connection between involvement and major gifts. But now we get to the problem we referred to in opening the chapter. Involvement demands a nonrenewable resource: time. Eric Sprott's views on time versus money were representative of many of our interviewees.

I have more money than time. And it's easier for me to give money than it is to spend the time. (I very much admire the people that spend the time, by the way.) So I try not to get deeply committed to spending time. My time is better spent doing what I do and have the fund get bigger and, you know, provide the money rather than the time.

For Larry Rosen, the preciousness of time, coupled with his desire to have impact, means he is very thoughtful about where to commit his involvement.

So I have to choose the time I dedicate to philanthropy carefully because when I join a board, I want to engage completely, and I want to make a difference.

Linda Frum looks at the issue from a slightly different point of view.

My feeling is that my plate is very full. I'm really busy, and I have way more to do than I have time to do. To add to that, to take on anything new, someone is really going to have to appeal to my philanthropic nature that says I can't say no. I feel everything is so overcrowded in my life. So to get involved, to give time, not just money, I have to be really passionate about what it is, I mean really passionate. The request has to come in a way that will stir those feelings.

In a previous chapter, we demonstrated that conveying a sense of passion was essential to winning financial support. If time is more valuable than money, it only stands to reason that, as Frum says, passion would also be the key to securing the involvement of the philanthropist.

We are left with a conundrum. Involvement leads to greater support, but philanthropists are often loath to part with the time that involvement requires. What to do?

In talking about her experience with the Zareinu Educational Centre and their annual fashion show, Frum offered what could be a viable solution to our challenge.

They were very smart. The first thing they ever asked of me was if I would emcee the event. I guess because I was emceeing, I gave $5,000 to be a sponsor. I didn't really know the organization very well, but the request was of my time to emcee. But when I got exposed to the event, it was beautiful, and I understood what they are trying to do. I came home and said, "We have to support this and send them a cheque." I had a long-term relationship with them because that event was so moving to me. Sometimes I think it's smart for *organizations to have a very low threshold to get people involved to get them in the door. Like to have an event that costs $50 or $75, even though they need millions of dollars. When things are so small and niche, you need to make yourself free and then hope the support follows. And that was the nature of that relationship with them. They asked me for very little up front. And the organization just sold itself.*

Making it easy to get involved is a plausible solution. But be careful not to miss what was at the heart of her story. Zareinu made it easy for her to get involved, but the organization also impressed the hell out of her. The combination of being an exemplary organization and creatively involving prospective donors is a good precursor to financial support.

The Reality of Giver Burnout

Giver burnout, which many volunteers and donors occasionally experience, was assumed to be the result of giving too much. The theory goes that if we sit on too many boards, write too many cheques, or spend too much time on our causes, we'll exhaust ourselves and need a break from the goodness.

Not so, say psychologists Olga Klimecki and Tania Singer. According to their research on caregivers, people don't develop burnout from giving too much; rather, when they sense their giving is not doing enough. Studies show that givers burn out when they do not see or feel the impact of their giving.[22]

12

*I know that half the money I spend on marketing is wasted;
the trouble is I don't know which half.*

—John Wanamaker

The Mystery of Marketing Material

Here's another interesting conundrum. Marketing collateral—brochures, reports, DVDs, and even websites and videos—appears to have almost no impact on the giving decisions of philanthropists, and yet most of them said that organizations must continue to produce them.

Honey Sherman

- Co-founder, with her husband Barry, of the Apotex Foundation
- Board member of York University, Mount Sinai Hospital, Baycrest Centre
- Former campaign chair of Toronto's UJA Federation
- Supporter of numerous educational and communal causes

For full bio, see page 139

Honey Sherman's views seem to sum up the riddle of marketing collateral. When asked what impact any of that material has on her giving decisions, she resolutely responded, "None." However, in discussing whether organizations should continue to invest in such material, she went on to say:

You've got to be out there. You send out a report because you [want people to] remember, "Oh, yeah, Baycrest," "Oh, yes, Save the Whales," "Oh, yeah, whatever." But there's no question that you must continue spending the time, effort, and energy, even as a piece of throwaway mail.

Richard Ivey articulated this dichotomy between personal behaviour and organizational imperative. It's hard to believe he could have been more forceful in discussing his personal views about marketing material.

I might leave it on a desk for a year or two, and then I throw it out. I rarely look at them. Never look at DVDs, never look at videos. Leave behinds do nothing for me.

But on the other hand, he was quick to endorse the use of such material.

In other organizations that I'm involved with, like CIFAR, we create brochures. Some people like them.

Don Johnson provided some insight into the role marketing collateral can play. "It gives [a campaign] credibility. It confirms that a lot of thought has gone into it." He then went on to confirm our paradox by telling us, "But me personally, I don't spend a whole lot of time reviewing the material. Some might. I personally go more by what they say at the meeting and how they respond to the questions."

Larry Rosen offered a very practical rationale for producing material. "It's good to have the material if it helps you understand the cause." Being even more specific, Philip Reichmann provided this perception: "Just sometimes you envision it wrong. Like you think that it is a little institution, and meanwhile, it has twelve buildings."

Gil Palter added to the discussion by pointing to the subliminal effect marketing material might have.

So we all think we're perfectly rational, but we're not. If somebody has a more compelling presentation—through whatever form of media they choose—whether I believe it or not, I know it's going to influence me.

For some, the effectiveness of marketing collateral was a function of its quality. Ed Sonshine had this to say.

The quality of it has some impact. Does it grab my interest? Is it going to be an event that RioCan can support? So in that sense, it can make a difference.

David Cynamon pointed out these issues of quality may not be unique to the philanthropic world. He references a recent request for funds.

He brought in really a first-class package from DVDs to high gloss to some really great articles, and the whole thing was really impressive. So I think the presentation for anything in life is critical.

Larry Kinlin equates collateral's lack of effectiveness with its general lack of quality. While ascribing the impact of publications as a "three out of ten," he says, "Most of them are not very good."

You might be tempted to think that the real problem is the quality of the material and that most collateral is ineffective because it's inferior. But our philanthropists had some serious reservations about the quest for marketing excellence.

Issy Sharp pointed out that "spending money for promotion can be a waste. If the cause is right, you don't need the bells and whistles."

While acknowledging the basic necessity of marketing material, Jim Fleck offered a caveat.

> You have to have material that presents well the case for whatever it is you're doing and gives the donor an idea of what the results will be. Sometimes if it's too glossy, it's a turnoff.

With views that are likely representative of many major givers, Martin Connell was strident when he said this:

> Less is best. Flashiness is a turnoff. It just smells of spending money that for all I can see, is for no good cause. It just makes me irritated to see that people would spend money on fancy brochures.

Connell hints at the fact that marketing material can in fact deter a donor from giving. Linda Frum took that thought one step further.

> Totally drives me crazy. Every time I get the stuff, I think, "What am I going to do with it?" It looks like it cost twenty dollars to produce, then someone has to courier it to me. I think, "Ugh, just give me an e-mail with your pitch," and that's all I need. Or a phone call conversation, but I do not need those materials. And again, they are a bit of a warning bell that it wasn't a great decision to spend money on that.

The implication is clear. If an organization is going to be unnecessarily extravagant in producing marketing material, will other spending decisions be likewise suspect?

For Naomi Azrieli, overspending on promotion goes beyond warning bells and right into the no-support category.

> There's one particular organization that I think spends so much money on their marketing that I think it's ridiculous and I can't support them. Why do that? Why spend your money on mailings and marketing material and all the rest of it?

Alex Shnaider

- Co-founder of the Midland Group, an international trading and investment holding company
- Benefactor of the Alex and Simona Shnaider Research Chair in Thyroid Oncology at Mount Sinai Hospital
- Supporter of numerous health care and communal organizations

For full bio, see page 139

Some philanthropists' feelings about marketing material are unconditionally negative. When asked if he had ever made a gift because of the quality of a video, brochure, or printed material, Alex Shnaider's response was resolute.

No, never. If anything, this causes me to wonder how much of my donation would go directly toward the cause and how much would be spent on marketing.

The one potential exception to the prevailing view of marketing material was related to websites and online communication. Gary Slaight told us, "If somebody sends me a really good e-mail with a link that I can click to without having to go look around, that can be effective."

Jay Hennick was even more emphatic. "I think the website is critical, but I think the rest of the stuff is a waste of money." Interestingly, when asked if a website alone has ever influenced him to give, he said, "Yes. If I go to a website and it's well put together and it explains exactly what the institution stands for, and it's fulsome, et cetera, it says to me that the institution is well organized." Perhaps mimicking the need for restraint expressed by others, he went on to say, "It doesn't have to be gorgeous. It just has to have succinct information about what that institution is." Finally, he draws the parallel to the business world. "If you want to know about that institution, it's just like if you're looking into a company. [The website is] critical."

Ed Sonshine very succinctly summed up the true role that marketing collateral plays when he said, "It's the ask that makes the difference, not the materials. The material is the backdrop for the ask."

Meaningful Versus Throwaway Materials

Years ago, Burnett Associates conceived a truly brilliant direct-mail pack for Amnesty International. It told the gruesome story of a young man who was tortured by having his eyes put out with an ordinary ballpoint pen. The mailing enclosed a small plastic pen and the copy read, "What you hold in your hand can be an instrument of torture, or it can change the world."

"Go on," the copy says of the small plastic pen that was attached. "Tear it off the page. Hold it in your hand. Feel the point. Think about it … Stretch your imagination. Because that's what torturers around the world do. They excel at it: using their imaginations to fashion instruments of torture out of the most everyday things."

Great copy—"Use the pen we've given you as an instrument of change, to change the world." After this proved to be one of the most effective direct-mail campaigns ever orchestrated, countless organizations started imitating the "pen idea." Regrettably, in most of these cases, all the meaning and relevance is lost.[22]

13

Research is formalized curiosity. It is poking and prying with a purpose.

—Zora Neale Hurston

The Catch-22 of Research

It seems obvious that conducting extensive research about a philanthropist is a necessary prerequisite to a successful solicitation. We discovered that philanthropists have strong, surprising, and often conflicted views about that research.

We asked philanthropists what they expected someone to know about them in advance of asking them for a major gift. Many were uncomfortable with being the subject of research. David Kassie's response was typical. "Hopefully as little as possible. I mean, seriously, it's not about me." Here's where it gets complicated because Kassie then went on to draw on his own experience to express the need for such research. "Look, I'm on a bunch of boards where I've organized meetings with five or ten wealthy CEOs to give either corporately or individually. And you know, a staff person would make a big deal about 'What's the angle?' So I get that. And I always get asked, 'What is the best way to approach someone?'"

Just to keep us on our toes, he returned to his previous views, but this time more decisively. "If anything, I don't think I would appreciate somebody figuring out that I did this, this, and this. What are you, a stalker?" Those are strong words and somewhat conflicting ideas. Kassie understands that effective fundraising requires good research but doesn't want anyone researching him.

Gil Palter took that feeling of discomfort to another level in describing how he wants to be unresearchable.

You know what? If you came in knowing nothing about me, I wouldn't be offended. I go to great lengths to stay below the radar screen. Every now and again, we do a transaction in the public markets that's big enough that they write about you whether you want them to or not. But I try to keep my head down and stay below the radar, so if you haven't been able to find out a lot about me, I'm not offended; I've tried to make it that way.

That might seem simple, except that Palter doesn't want his time wasted with opportunities that are outside his areas of interest.

We've taken the time over a large number of years to define what's in the box and what's not in the box. I cut people off really quickly. I'm not going to spend the hour with you if your five-minute overview of what you're doing is clearly outside of the box.

Martin Connell's sophisticated views on the topic provide the resolution to the catch-22 of the philanthropist who says, "Don't research me, but present me with options in which I'm likely to be interested." Here's what Connell had to say about whether a solicitor should know his giving history:

No, in fact, the more they know, or the more they let on they know, the more paranoid I become. So I don't want them to tell me everything about myself because it feels like I'm overly researched, and that sort of unsettles me. I don't mind somebody saying, "I know you're interested in microfinance" or whatever; if they read it, that's fine. But be subtle! And don't go overboard. Don't be a smarty-pants. Because if you are, I think you can irritate people.

In other words, "Do your research, but just don't let me know that you've done it."

Many philanthropists were adamant in expressing the opposite point of view and expected fundraisers to have done their homework. Donald Johnson expressed that sentiment and explained the consequences of not doing the research.

I expect them to know a lot. If they have not really done a lot of research, why do they think I would have an interest in their cause? What are my giving patterns? What have I supported previously, and why would I have an interest—because of me, my family, or a close friend? If they have not done the research, I tend to make it a short conversation.

For Johnson, it's almost a matter of principle. If you respect him and his time, you must be prepared. Aubrey Dan concurred with Johnson but went on to look at the issue more pragmatically.

If somebody doesn't do that [research] on the organization's side, then the odds of success are dramatically lower. If you're just throwing stuff against the wall [saying], "I've got a wonderful cause," well, guess what? Line up; there's thousands of people … So it really is finding out [about the philanthropist], and you almost need a private investigator to get the history of a particular person to see how they grew up, what were their challenges, and how to find one or two multiple hooks. If you don't do that, then it's strictly random.

Dan was among many philanthropists who de-personalized the matter and simply saw it as a matter of effectiveness. Joe Lebovic had this opinion:

Joe Lebovic

- Owner, Lebovic Enterprises Limited, a land development and construction company
- Board member of many nonprofit organizations
- Principal supporter of the Joseph and Wolf Lebovic Health Complex at Mount Sinai Hospital
- Benefactor of the Joseph & Wolf Lebovic Community Campus
- Supporter of numerous other communal and health-related causes

For full bio, see page 135

First of all, when you go to somebody, you have to understand his background. You have to understand what he's giving, why he's giving and to see how you can get him involved and that what you want is something similar with what he has been doing.

Jim Fleck has probably solicited as many gifts as he's given. He believes that research is not just important but in fact the *key* to effective fundraising. In talking about the industry, he said this:

University of Toronto is the most effective fundraising organization. Jon Dellandrea (University of Toronto's former chief advancement officer) said once that if he had a little more money, he wouldn't hire another solicitor; he would hire another researcher. Getting very good research on the people you're approaching is important. First of all, it helps to unearth what the hooks might be, and it also helps on the capacity side.

Gerald Halbert

- Board member, Toronto General & Western Hospital Foundation, along with a host of other health-related and communal organizations
- Member, Governing Council, University of Toronto
- Member, Order of Canada

For full bio, see page 129

When asked what the secret to a good solicitation is, his response reiterated the need for research. "It's finding a hook—which isn't a secret. It's finding a reason why they should give to this particular thing versus ten others. That's all."

Gerald Halbert is another philanthropist who is a very experienced solicitor. He sees research largely in terms of assessing giving capacity.

> *You cannot go and ask someone for an amount that is way out of line. So you've got to do your homework before you ask. Who are these people? What is their background? You're not going to go and ask someone for $50,000 when an excellent gift for that individual would be $5,000 or $10,000. It's embarrassing to a person.*

For Richard Ivey, the importance of research cannot be overstated, and the bounds of that research are frighteningly limitless.

> *You really have to do your homework when you make those calls and really find your angle. I don't make a call to someone without ten pages of research, and I know every school that you burped or farted at. I've got quotes from every speech they have ever given that are relevant to the organization. I know what their wife does. I know every cheque they have ever written, and I look for little tiny angles to get their attention.*

As Ivey points out, research isn't always about what causes the donor has supported and in what amounts. Every aspect of the donor's attitudes, preferences, and interests should be considered.

Good research isn't limited to what gets done in advance of the first meeting. It can continue throughout the stewardship process and has the potential to demonstrate leadership as well as add context to subsequent gift requests. Kelly Meighen sees ongoing research as being essential to the successful development of a relationship with an organization.

> *As the process goes along, I think, as a donor or a potential donor, I should always be surprised. They should always be one step ahead of me. Because what does that say to me? That they're on top of it, they're strategic, they're thinking. So I don't think research is as important at the beginning of the process, but it's certainly important as you go along ...*

And does that research pay off? Meighen described two instances that conclusively demonstrated the effectiveness of good ongoing research. The first was focused on the development of the Meighen Foundation's relationship with the University of Western Ontario.

They ultimately came to us with a proposal to support graduate students in the faculty of engineering. And my father was the first dean of engineering at Western. They had gone into the faculty archives and found speeches that my dad had written and given. And [they] had determined there was a theme apparently of environmental sustainability. My dad was appointed dean in 1961, so this was a long time ago. And part of the package—the ask—were these speeches with highlights about his obvious interest, which I never knew about. In 1960, I was quite a little person. So that created the focus for the scholarships, and you know, not only did I take it to the [foundation] board, but I took it to my mother and to my sisters [for us to support it personally].

The second experience that Kelly told us about makes a good case for listening as an effective form of research. As Kelly puts it, "If someone listens very well, that is the key as far as I'm concerned because, if you listen, you pick up keys about who you are talking to."

It's Meighen's encounters with the Canadian Association for Mental Health (CAMH) that makes the case for this listening-based research.

She described how she was taken on a tour of an older mental health facility and found it disturbing. As the visit continued, Kelly expressed her views about what she was seeing, at one point saying, "And we call ourselves a civil society, and this is the way we treat people who are no longer able to understand."

The fundraisers at CAMH were obviously paying attention. "And somebody was listening. So when I got the ask for a donation toward the redevelopment at CAMH, they didn't use my exact words, but they had the theme. They had the kernel and the framework for a tailor-made presentation and ask to us."

Both of Meighen's experiences demonstrate sophisticated research approaches that worked rather well.

What happens in the absence of good research? The results can be insulting to the donor and embarrassing to the one asking for a gift. David Cynamon spoke generally about the need to research a prospective donor's experiences with the organization that is asking for support.

If somebody had a horrible experience with that particular institution or foundation and they are still getting called upon by a fundraiser and that person didn't know about the bad experience, that would maybe insult [the donor], and he might say, "Why are you here? Didn't you know that a year ago?"

Going from the theoretical to the practical, he went on to describe a difficult experience of his own.

> *I had that situation at a health care institution. And it was me at the other end asking for a gift, and I didn't know that the person I was asking had a very bad experience with their late mother at the institution and that I shouldn't have gone there. And I could see it being obviously important, at least on the philanthropic side, to know whether they had good experiences or bad with the organization.*

If it's essential that organizations research prospective donors, the reverse may be true as well. Julia Koschitzky first expounded on her expectation of what a solicitor will know about her.

> *I think nowadays there's no excuse for people not to know about you because anybody can be Googled. I think it's very important for you to know about the person [you are asking for a gift]. That's the research that you have to do.*

Then, in discussing a meeting she had with someone raising funds for a local political candidate, she said, "And actually, I did the same because the night before I met him, I had to find out who this guy is."

Those soliciting gifts would be wise to take heed of Julia Koschitzky's modus operandi. If, as our interviews demonstrated, research is invaluable to those asking, it may be of equal import to those being asked.

Donors Should Also Do Research

In a 2010 major donor survey conducted by Hope Consulting, a San Francisco–based philanthropy advisory firm, "organizational effectiveness" was the most cited factor in choosing a charity, identified by 90 percent of surveyed givers. Yet when the Hope Consulting team began to look at the actual behaviour of these very same donors, an entirely different picture emerged. While the vast majority of donors say they care about charitable effectiveness, few make serious efforts to confirm it. Fully 65 percent of donors confess that they never do any research.

Donors say about half of their research is drawn from the charity itself, either by looking at its website or by talking to one of its volunteers or employees, and opinions of friends and family stand second. Thus, as well meaning as those donors may be, their research veers heavily toward the anecdotal and subjective.[23]

14

Beware of the person who can't be bothered by details.

—William Feather

Vision Matters — but Details Matter More

There is no question that major gifts are often made on the basis of a compelling vision. While that vision may be key to getting the gift, delivering on detail will keep the donor. Philanthropists want to be inspired. Without results, however, their trust fades, and their interest wanes. In the world of fundraising, sweating the small stuff will reap big rewards.

Many times, it is the donor, and not the organization, that brings the vision to the table.

Jay Hennick's first major gift was based on a personal vision of creating the means for law students to also acquire an MBA. His strong conviction was that the combination of an MBA and a law degree was the best possible preparation for business success. He was prepared to back up his belief and to create the Jay Hennick JD/MBA Program, which would provide the funds to allow those with a law degree to spend an additional year and get their MBAs.

The project was ultimately mired in procedure and politics and was never brought to fruition in the way Hennick had visualized it. Hennick's second attempt to establish a JD/MBA program was at another university and also did not meet his expectations.

Although Hennick brought his personal convictions to each of these institutions, once the gift was accepted, the organization effectively took ownership of the mission, as well as the obligation to fulfill it. Hennick has sound advice for donors and organizations involved in these situations.

> *That's what donors should do on larger gifts. They should say to the institution, "First of all, if you don't believe in what I'd like to transform, then don't do it. But if you believe in it and you think it would be great for the institution, go do a business plan. I'm happy to critique it, but I'm going to want to build in metrics and you pick them. You tell me what metrics you need to measure your own success. I just need to know every year that you're on track as far as you're concerned.*

Aubrey and Marla Dan had a vision for the way in which a seniors' facility could meet the needs of its residents.

> *I would say specifically the building is for those people who are sixty-five and older and are independent. They may need a caregiver, but, while they're elderly, they feel young and active. So the vision there, the original vision, was that there was going to be social and wellness programs. That was part of the deal. Part of our gift was specifically to fund that.*

On that basis, they established a fund that would specifically enable that programming.

Many years later, the programs are still not there. The Dans are saddened by what they see as a missed opportunity. In Aubrey's words, "And that's disappointing because we see so much of the value of what could be there, and it's not happening, unfortunately."

They are also frustrated because the funding to implement the programming still exists. As Marla explains, "There's still a lot of funds there, and they're not using it the way that they [agreed to]." Discussions about how to use the proceeds of the fund reveal a further disconnect between the Dans and the organization. "So [the money] sits there, and they come back and ask us for it to be used for other purposes, and we say, 'No, that's not what it's supposed to be used for.'"

Aubrey comes to a decidedly business-based conclusion. "The parameters of the business model have never been adhered to. So management fundamentally never delivered on what it promised."

On the basis of this experience and others, the Dans are circumspect when considering a relationship with an organization. Aubrey details the elements of their due diligence. "[We] look at the organization, look at their track record of what they've delivered, talk to multiple donors, find out if they are happy. What's their ratio of [support] in fact going to the end user, and what's their admin-cost ratio?"

One might think that because of the complicated repercussions of large donations, most philanthropists become cynical or stoic about their giving. So it was often heartening to see that those who have spent so much of their lives involved in philanthropy could still be motivated by a compelling vision. In describing his reasons for supporting the Toronto International Film Festival, and then becoming its first board chair, Martin Connell used these terms:

> It had very little to do with how I was asked, and it was very much about what the promise was. What was the promise? The promise was to create a film festival that would draw the best films from around the world, showcase them in Toronto, show them on an annual basis, and do it for the betterment of bringing good films to people.

Don't think that because Connell can be inspired, he abandons a penchant for the practical. In fact, in his advice to new fundraisers, he draws a strong link between vision and implementation.

> There is definitely a need for clarity of purpose, clarity of vision, and a really concrete business plan. That's the starting point. If you don't have that, it's going to be really, really tough. And make sure the purpose and the cause is realistic and fits the reality of the world we live in. It's not some goofy, far-off idea; it's really grounded in the practical. If it's grounded in the practical, you have a much better chance.

Attention to detail can be an effective method of soliciting a gift in the first place. The scale model of a development, the edited photo with the donor's name on the side of the building, or the mock-up of the recognition plaque are all examples of these techniques. David Cynamon was among those donors who saw the benefit of being provided with detail in early stages. Here's what he had to say.

> The best presentations are, for me, the ones that I can visualize the finished version of whatever the project is. May it be brick-and-mortar, may it be books, may it be education, however they can best [allow me to] visualize that. You almost want them to bring a model in if that's going to be what you're inevitably going to build because everybody wants to feel and touch it.

There are times when a connection is based on personal experience that provides a vision for the impact an organization can have. Brendan Calder's experience is a good example.

> *The people from Outward Bound knock[ed] on my door. I've done four Outward Bounds. I've been to Banff. They figured that out. I got a lot out of Outward Bound. They asked me [for a gift], and I haven't done it, but maybe I will one of these days. So I'm already predisposed.*

It sounded like a happy ending was imminent—at least until Calder's desire for detail came to the fore. "But not until I can feel that [a gift] really has impact do I even go to the next step." Ironically, Calder used the words of someone he had solicited for a gift to explain his own feelings about Outward Bound. "I was asking somebody for money the other day, and he said, 'What I won't do is put money into a black box and hope you use it well because you think it is a great cause. I've got to see where the money is going to and see the effect of it over and over again.'"

The vision can often be broader—reaching beyond a particular initiative or organization. We have already discussed how Carlo Fidani uses his philanthropic giving as a means to foster the ideal of collaboration within the health care sector. His passion is evident as he expounds on his view.

> *The days of us fighting the notion of silos are gone. The days of working in isolation are gone because they are unsustainable on a financial level, and the days of collaboration are upon us. I think the best way to place your bet or your gift is on the opportunity that provides an intersection of the greatest number of collaborations or collaborators.*

But there is a caveat. True collaboration can't be left to chance, and it is the detail that will be the determinant of success. Fidani explains, "The system has to be engineered. Otherwise, you get all sorts of fighting, and you can actually create problems rather than solve them." Stepping back a little, Fidani provides some overall advice to other philanthropists considering a particular project. "You have to research it, you have to understand it, you have to know who your partners are, and you have to know what that gift means at the time."

Sometimes it's the philanthropist that provides the attention to detail. Organizations would be wise to heed the lesson inherent in what Aditya Jha told us.

Aditya Jha

• Former Chairman and CEO of Karma Candy, and founder of several successful software companies
•Founder of POA Educational Foundation.
• Member and officer, Order of Canada
• Supporter of many educational, aboriginal, and human rights causes

For full bio, see page 131

One day, I was going to give a $40,000 cheque to UNICEF Canada. I had a guy who was working as a fundraising professional in my car, and he told me I should park near a particular office. I was going round and round, and finally I found a place and parked. When we were walking to the office, he asked, "Why did you park there?" I said, "You see, it's four dollars cheaper." He said, "I don't understand. You're giving $40,000, and you're worried about $4?" I said, "That's why I worry when I hear these kind of things from you. I am just worried what you will do with my money."

Lawrence Bloomberg has also made health care a focus of his philanthropy. He sees it as a means of fulfilling his larger aim of "wanting to be actively involved in making society better." More specifically, Bloomberg explained, "To me, nothing seemed to be as important as health care. Health care was an area that was changing so much that individual businesspeople could play an important role and help the management at these institutions do a better job."

Despite the lofty vision, Bloomberg maintains detail-oriented expectations.

Sometimes, before you make a gift, you'll lay out what metrics—what goals—you expect to achieve. We live in a world where accountability has become everything. I mean, in health care, it is all about accountability today and measurement, making everything very open. If you can't measure it, how do you know you're doing any good?

Philanthropists sometimes used visionary terms to describe their overall rationale for giving. Larry Tanenbaum's philosophy was an example. "We were inspired by all of our gifts because that's what philanthropy should be about: to be inspired by it and it inspires you." Yet that principled approach to philanthropy doesn't blind Tanenbaum to the need for organizations to deliver on detail.

I always ask for an accountability of what is being done with our money. If it is a yearly donation, I want to know how did last year's do and what are you going to be doing with next year's. If it is an endowment, there are certain criteria we set up that define to what projects the proceeds automatically go, but there have to be certain standards set to make sure [those criteria] are followed and the endowment continues on.

In fact, the metrics of accountability were most frequently the way in which philanthropists expressed the need for a detailed approach. Gerry Schwartz's views were typical.

> *Well, there is not a return on an investment or a return on invested capital or that kind of measurement device, but there are other metrics. We measure hours of community service by our students; I measure the development of the IT center at Mount Sinai emergency department trying to develop a system to be used hopefully around the world to make the incoming patients go through the process more efficiently and the doctors handle it more pleasantly and effectively. There are all kinds of measurements. We track it. We are careful about it. As I said, we have an eleven-person board, nine of whom are independent. We report to them pretty clearly on each program—what it was designed to do, what it has done.*

It's interesting that Schwartz's riff on metrics actually included his vision for what could be achieved through funding improvements to the IT system at Mount Sinai Hospital. It speaks to the symbiotic, or even existential, relationship between vision and metrics. Without metrics, the realization of a vision remains unproved, and without a vision, it's not clear what is to be measured.

Facing the Consequences of Disappointment

After witnessing her husband fall victim to alcoholism, Adele Smithers-Fornaci became one of the most significant supporters of alcohol abuse treatment. She committed her life to educating people about alcoholism and made large gifts in support of research and treatment. In 1994, when the Smithers Alcoholism Treatment and Training Center at Saint Luke's Roosevelt Hospital began using endowed funds for purposes other than those for which they were designated, she sued for return of her multi-million-dollar gift. By winning the case, Smithers-Fornaci set a precedent for other donors to legally enforce the terms of their gifts.

Six years later, when learning that Saint Luke's was conducting a controversial "moderation" treatment, Smithers-Fornaci was even more furious and took out full-page ads in the New York Times criticizing the hospital as putting more people at risk. The hospital was eventually pressured to cancel the program.[24]

15

You can only get what is yours by giving the other person what is his.

—Wallace D. Wattles

Reciprocity has its Limits

The quid pro quo is a well-established tenet of doing business. Enterprise and its relationships thrive on reciprocity. That dynamic certainly has its place in the world of philanthropy, but—as we discovered—it's not without its caveats and limitations.

For Issy Sharp, it's a very simple principle. "So you invite a hundred people here to a charitable event, bet your bottom dollar when they have something, they will ask you to come too, and you'll have to go."

Gary Slaight is rather emphatic about the appropriateness of reciprocity.

> *If somebody has given me money and then they come and ask me for money, am I likely to do it? Are you talking about scratching each other's back? It happens, for sure. I will say to people, "If you want ... I'll exchange cheques with you. Absolutely."*

Can reciprocity lead to a large gift? While Kelly Meighen feels more obliged at lower levels, it would certainly appear that philanthropic mutuality can bring big bucks to an organization.

> *I do feel compelled at the lower end. A friend of ours is the chair for the TSO [Toronto Symphony Orchestra]. So, do we buy tickets for the gala? That's supporting a friend. Is the door open when the TSO comes to talk about the possibility of a gift? Absolutely. [It is open] where it might not be otherwise. I*

used the TSO as an example because I think we gave $150,000 to the TSO for education to bring kids to the symphony. It was not a huge gift. I don't think we would have done that if we hadn't been friends with the woman who was the chair.

While the organization is often its beneficiary, reciprocity is, at its core, deeply personal. The willfulness is palpable in Jay Hennick's comments about becoming chair of the UJA Federation campaign.

But every time I wrote a cheque, I kept track. And I've got a whole file there of every dollar I've given to every person over the years, and it's almost $2 million. I'm going back to every [person] ... and I'm actually looking forward to it. Because if I gave you money, and you say no [to me], you're off the f— — list. Forever.

A story told by Ed and Fran Sonshine illustrates how personal the principal of reciprocity can be.

We've been supporting a particular organization for a very long time. And not so much that we are madly in love with it. It wasn't a huge thing, but it was fairly significant—$10,000 a year for about seven or eight years. And basically, it was because of the person who was asking. Then we were working on another project that was very important to us. So we went to this person and, out of reciprocity, asked for support for our program. And the comment that came back was, "It's not in our budget this year," and [she] didn't give us anything. It was curt and horrible. And I don't think she realized what she'd done. She does now. Then this woman came back to us because it was time for the organization [for which she is raising money], and I could not even look at her. I was so angry that she had the nerve to come back to us for our yearly $10,000 when she didn't have ten cents to give to this other organization that we were working on. She didn't get it. Didn't get it at all, and she lost us. It's gone. Really... I mean, a good organization, but the only reason we gave her money was because she was asking.

Coining a great phrase, Larry Rosen defines the payback dynamic as "What goes around gives around." He uses what appear to be real-life situations to illustrate the interpersonal obligations of philanthropy.

When you go to somebody and say, "Buy a $25,000 table for an event honouring my father," when they come to you the next year and say, "I'm working for the

Alzheimer Society. Buy a $10,000 table," you don't have much defense. So the reality is that asking comes back at you, but you just have to do it.

Reciprocity can be viewed as the by-product of a healthy community of givers. Consider Linda Frum's comments:

Usually, if a very good friend of mine asks me to do something, I will accommodate them. I'm very proud to live in a community that's very philanthropic, so everybody is asking everybody else. You just have to be available. There's no chance that I can say no to a very good friend that has been supportive of me. Just does not work. In a way, it makes it easy, though.

Her last sentence points to an otherwise hidden dimension of back-scratching. It makes giving decisions easy. You don't have to ponder the merits of an organization when you feel an obligation to the person asking.

Martin Connell also sees the communal raison d'être of reciprocity but interestingly raises the rhetorical question of what would exist in its absence.

I think it is a reasonable assumption that there is a high level of reciprocity. But what would happen if we all just stayed home and looked after our favourite charity? I think it would probably just be a wash. I think it's part of the reality of living in a diverse community where you've got lots of things going on, and we all need help, and we all want to help. So it makes sense.

Maybe it's not just a matter of exchanging gifts. For Gerry Schwartz, philanthropists are often trading in trust.

If I go to Mr. X, ask him to consider a donation, and he makes a meaningful one to an organization that I've brought to his attention, [when] he comes to see me later for something he's interested in, just like he trusted my recommendation, I am very inclined to trust his recommendation.

There are spheres where reciprocity doesn't take a financial form but rather makes demands on one's time. Eric Lindros introduced us to the philanthropic payback of professional athletes and its challenges.

Where it'll get crazy is a lot of times some guys have charities in their own names. So they would bring in a pile of guys to go to the [golf] tournament, but it got to the point where everybody had a tournament. Then everybody had to go to everybody's tournament. They are all great causes, but there has to be a balance in life, as well.

Being an integral part of a cadre of givers can have a negative tinge. Take David Cynamon's views, for example:

> Number one, I think you're going to give to an institution, to a cause, to an individual who has been very supportive of you. The more you put yourself into that position, the more you can expect to be solicited and expect to give. And until you're ready to get off that carousel of asking, don't expect to get off the carousel of giving. It's just a vicious circle.

His use of the carousel was a pithy analogy, and its endless quality rang true with a number of philanthropists. Just because you feel obligated doesn't mean you like it.

There are, of course, limitations to just how much the payback principle will work. Sometimes the organization has to stand on its own merits. James Fleck provided that perspective.

> [The prospect] should be making a large gift to something I'm soliciting on the basis of the inherent value of the project and its usefulness and not on the basis of me.

Being as much a fundraiser as a giver, Fleck eloquently summed up reciprocity's potential. "It opens the door, but it doesn't close the sale."

There were philanthropists for whom reciprocity was not a factor in their decision making. Incredibly, Brendan Calder's philanthropy has never been touched by the obligation of mutual support. This is what he had to say:

> No one has ever come back to me and said, "Hey, I gave you money for that, and you should give me money for this." And I've certainly given and been solicited, but it never occurred to me to go back and ask for something quid pro quo.

Could the preparedness to have one's giving be governed by this payback principle in fact be a generational issue? According to Gil Palter, it is.

> I have found that the generation ahead of me are very much into the "You scratch my back, I'll scratch your back" with regard to philanthropy. I care about this cause, so you give to it, and then when you come and ask me about the cause you care about, I'll give to that.

Palter and his wife Elisa are very thoughtful about their giving, and doing it based simply on an IOU does not compute. For them, solicitations based on reciprocity even border on the offensive.

> *And so when people come to us and are raising money for something that falls completely outside of our sphere of interest in philanthropic strategy and twist our arm to give because they're giving and link it to something like "I'm a customer of your business" or whatever the case may be, I react very poorly to that.*

Does Palter put those principles into practice? You bet he does.

> *I never solicit that way. I always solicit based on something that I find compelling and important and tell donors, "Here are the reasons why [I'm supporting this cause], and if you share my feelings towards that, if this resonates with you as a cause we're supporting, I'd love to talk to you about a gift.*

The views of Palter, Calder, and Fleck are exceptions to the rule of reciprocity that is clearly a significant factor in the giving decisions of most philanthropists. However, it's also evident that it has its limitations, particularly as it relates to the size of a gift. Reciprocity may open the door to a relationship with a donor, but, as Jim Fleck would say, to "close the sale" on a major gift is going to take far more.

The Quid Pro Quo of Fundraising

Since he retired from Family Dollar in 2003, Leon Levine has transferred his man-on-the-scene approach in business to the foundation that bears his name.

"Leon's gone after philanthropy in much the same way as he did making money," said Hugh L. McColl Jr., former chief executive of Bank of America, which is based in Charlotte. "He sees donations as investments in worthwhile projects, he does a lot of due diligence when looking at potential recipients, and he's diligent about holding their feet to the fire about doing what the money is supposed to do."

So it came as no surprise when Mr. McColl, after soliciting Mr. Levine to participate in an arts campaign in 2010, was presented with a counteroffer, a quid pro quo. Mr. Levine would make a sizable donation to the arts campaign if Mr. McColl would help raise funds for an antipoverty initiative. "Typical Leon negotiating tactics," Mr. McColl said.

Those tactics have been a boon for Charlotte during a difficult time. The $83 million arts campaign was a success, resulting in the renaming of a prominent new museum and theatre complex as the Levine Center for the Arts. And the poverty initiative raised millions during a recession that had rocked the Southeastern banking capital especially hard.[25]

16

We made too many wrong mistakes.

—Yogi Berra

Gifts Gone Wrong

It's not shocking to discover that philanthropic projects don't always work out as planned. The surprise is that, even though there may be millions of dollars involved, donations are rarely revoked. The further revelation is that a botched project most often doesn't lead to the demise of the relationship between the philanthropist and the organization.

We may find this hard to believe because we implicitly think of philanthropic commitments as we would a business deal. But as Naomi Azrieli so astutely points out, philanthropy is not always like business.

> *In business, you can always pull out. You can say, "I'm not in with you anymore," or "I lost money; I'm out," or "I made money, but not enough," or just "I'm done with you." Actually, when you make a donation, it's gone. You can't get it back, not under Canada Revenue Agency rules or any other rules. It's gone.*

Most often, gifts gone wrong are the result of poor management and a lack of attention to the donor's needs. Sometimes, it's almost unbelievable how badly organizations fare at each of those. Here's a cautionary tale from Kelly Meighen.

The Meighen Foundation made a gift to a midsized Canadian university that was known for its very comprehensive support services for students with disabilities. The result was going to be the Meighen Centre, a facility dedicated to students with learning disabilities. Kelly provides some perspective on the significance of the donation.

> *It was the first million-dollar gift we ever gave. And that was a huge amount*
> *of money in those days. A huge amount of money a) for our foundation, and*
> *b) for the university.*

The first inkling of trouble came when the Meighens were invited to attend an event at which they were going to be publicly thanked for this landmark contribution. Meighen picks up the story.

> *So we get down there, and we discover that we're actually not the only ones*
> *that are getting honoured. We are kind of co-honourees with some guy who*
> *has been a science professor for [many] years. Well, I felt sorry for him because*
> *he'd given his academic life to [the university], and he had to share the stage*
> *with us. It was totally improper for him and for us.*

That certainly wasn't a great exercise in stewardship. At the very least, the Meighens should have been told that they were going to share the spotlight. The story only gets worse from there.

> *They kept talking about this huge boost we'd given the university and that the*
> *Meighen Centre was going to be the cornerstone of strategic plans going*
> *forward and what would we do without the Meighen Centre and blah blah*
> *blah. But three years later, they were having a capital campaign, and I was*
> *asked to go listen to the plans for the campaign, and all I'd been hearing about*
> *the last three years was this gab about the Meighen Centre and what would*
> *we do without you. So we all reviewed the strategic initiatives that were being*
> *covered by this campaign, and I put up my hand and said, "What about the*
> *Meighen Centre—you know, we're the cornerstone of the university?"*

How is this possible? A university accepts a major gift to establish a centre for those with learning disabilities, and three years later, it's not part of their future financial planning. The untold element is that the million-dollar gift was an endowment. The cost of running the centre was going to have come from operating funds and the small amount of interest generated by the endowment.

As Kelly explains, "They were hugely underfunded. Still, a million [dollars] was a lot of money, but it only throws off $35,000 a year. You can't run a centre on that kind of money, and when I asked to see the university's budget, I didn't see anything [being directed at] the Meighen Centre."

The university should likely have determined whether they could afford to operate the centre before accepting the gift. Even if we give them the benefit of the doubt and assume that they believed it was within their budget but circumstances subsequently changed, they should have communicated that to the Meighens. The end result was a donor who felt taken advantage of and was ready to give up. As Meighen said, "So we kind of said to ourselves, 'Okay, that's it for [the university]; we're done.'"

Unbelievably, perhaps, this was not the end of the road. Kelly explains, "And it took them a long time and a lot of persuading and cajoling and talking and apologizing and saying, 'Can we start over?' to get us back. And we weren't inclined for a long time."

Notwithstanding all of the above, funding continued, and the Meighen Centre is still a part of this university. Kelly's reflection on what transpired zeroes in on the real issues.

> It's not that we were dying to be centre stage at a luncheon. That's not the point. The point is, we felt like we were sold a bill of goods. And, in fact, they talked, but they didn't back it up with their own financial commitment.

As previously mentioned, Jay Hennick's seven-figure gift to one university also led to a disgruntled donor. Jay tells the story of what he remarkably still describes as his most meaningful philanthropic gift.

> I made a large gift—at least, at the time, it was a large gift for me. It was the biggest gift the university had ever got, and it was a stretch for me, and the idea was to create the Hennick JD/MBA, and it was really money to fund students to take an extra year. If they were law students, they wouldn't have to pay for the business courses but would have to dedicate a year of their time to get a business degree.

It didn't work out as planned. Even though the faculty accepted the gift with Hennick's clear intention, internal strife and other factors prevented the realization of Hennick's dream. This is Jay's description of what resulted.

> The result was, I've honoured my pledge and allowed them to give the money on an annual basis to students that did anything else in terms of additive education. So if they wanted to go do their LLM, I would pay for it. If they wanted to do a US law degree, I would pay for it.

Hang on a minute. He made his gift to enable those with law degrees to get an MBA, but in the end, it got watered down so that it was funding any additional education and not just MBAs. Incredibly, he honoured his pledge—but not without second thoughts, as he explains. "What I really should have done is said, 'Give me back my money.' But I didn't feel that was the right thing to do."

How did the folks at the university salvage the situation? Hennick makes that clear.

> And so they acknowledged their own mistake right away, and they thanked me for not revoking the balance of the pledge and allowing them to allocate the money to other people that they consider to be worthy. They asked me whether I wanted to be involved in the selection process. And whenever there is a function, whenever the president of the university is going to be in Toronto, whenever the head of the law school is in Toronto, they reach out in a nice way ... you know, they say, "Would love to see you if you have the time."

What's truly notable is that this is a case where even though a multimillion-dollar gift went wrong, the donor not only maintained his relationship but would look favourably on future giving opportunities. This is the explanation that Jay, in his no-nonsense style, provides:

> The university [is an] example where I had a bad experience with execution, yet they do so many wonderful things to maintain the donor relationship, and I would give them money again, even though they screwed up on my program.

Sydney Cooper

- Former president and CEO, Pitts Engineering Construction Ltd.
- Director on the boards of many corporations and nonprofit organizations
- Former president, Technion Canada and supporter of numerous health- and business-related causes

For full bio, see page 125

Here's an example where donated funds were used for something that was completely different from the purpose for which the donor made the gift. Incredibly, it didn't end the relationship with the philanthropist.

Sydney Cooper talked about making a substantial gift to an organization. "They were building the big building they're in now. We gave [them] money specifically for a gymnasium. This was going to be their Cooper Gymnasium."

Reasonably, he wanted to see what his contribution had built. "And about a year or two later, we go up there, and we met with them and said, 'Show us what you've done.' So we walked down below to go see this gymnasium, and there's no gymnasium—no gymnasium. [They] built a library instead."

What was Cooper's reaction? Probably not what most would imagine. "Now we were a little annoyed by it, but again, it was kind of funny. [The organization] said, 'We needed a library; we didn't need a gymnasium.' I said, 'You could have come to us. We would have said yes.'"

It's hard to believe that the organization didn't lose Cooper as a donor. Certainly, a business arrangement in which one party made that kind of change wouldn't have ended amicably. Cooper frames the incident as a matter of accountability. "So specifically, you want to see what you're committed to being done." But he's quick to then point to the unique relationship with the fundraiser for the organization. "But you can't get mad at the guy. He comes here, and he's got one quip or another. And we get invited to their dinners." The personal respect and affection that Cooper had for the fundraiser compensated for what otherwise could have been a fatal fundraising error.

Our last account demonstrates that philanthropists truly appreciate it when organizations facing a derailed project take the high road. This is Richard Ivey's narrative:

> The [Ivey] Foundation gave money to [a hospital] once. I am guessing $100,000. We wrote a cheque for $32,000 for the first year, and we didn't really hear from them for a couple of years. So we wrote them a letter asking them what the hell was going on, and they replied that they'd cancelled the project and gave us back the rest of our money. What had happened was the researcher had left that was going to be working on that project, and nobody else was interested in it or capable of doing it.

Ivey's succinct analysis is spot-on. "It's a story you do not hear very often, but it is the right thing to do." His resultant advice to organizations is as accurate as it is to the point. "Give me the money back if you are going down a different road."

It's clear that not all organizations have heeded Ivey's advice. It's also evident that even when they don't, if the relationship is healthy, odds are pretty good that they'll keep the money and the philanthropist.

Taking It All Back

A famous philanthropic dispute involved a $20 million gift that Lee Bass, from Fort Worth, Texas, made to his alma mater, Yale College, to fund an extensive course in Western civilization. Because of its scope, the course necessitated hiring some new professors. As the donor, Bass figured he should have something to say in the selection, and in particular, he wanted to be sure that the new professors weren't, in his opinion, too politically correct or liberal. Yale firmly believed that it was entitled to choose its own faculty without interference. After a tense, four-year standoff, the conflict could not be resolved, and Yale returned the money—and not without some embarrassment to both sides, as both bore responsibility for the gift having to be taken back so publicly.[26]

17

*Failure is instructive. The person who really thinks learns quite
as much from his failures as from his successes.*

—John Dewey

How Not to Get the Gift

Most of this book is focused on best practices for achieving fundraising and philanthropic success. But in our interviews with philanthropists, we were told about some experiences that represent just the opposite. In the spirit of learning from our collective mistakes, in this chapter, we present sure-fire techniques for fundraising failure.

Insensitivity

Previously, we presented some thoughts on generational differences in attitudes to philanthropy. David Kassie's experience demonstrates how some generational and gender-related perceptions can lead to disaster.

> *When I was much younger ... a guy who was in my industry canvassed me on a hospital donation. This was one of the first pitches that I had ever received asking me to donate a lot of money. And I said to him, "Okay, look, it's a hospital that I have a lot of affinity for. Let me talk to my wife. You know we make our decisions together." He said, "Who wears the pants in your family anyways?" So I started laughing and said, "I can see for your generation that that might be the case, but in mine, this is a relationship." And he said, "Oh, fine. What's her number? Let me talk to her." So I gave him her number, and he actually called her. After [my wife] said to him, "Well, that's a lot of money," he said, "Well, what do you care? It's not your money, anyway."*

There was great potential for success in the solicitation. Kassie said this was an institution for which he had affinity. In addition, he didn't balk at the request for a major gift. He wanted to speak to his wife. That might even have been a positive indication. But through unimaginable insensitivity, the solicitor turned what could easily have been a successful call into a dismal failure.

Organizational Conflict and Indecision

Organizational infighting is a great way to drive away donors. When asked about any negative philanthropic experiences, Hal Jackman recalled a failed attempt from the 1980s to build a combined ballet and opera centre.

> *I chaired the campaign for the original ballet and opera house, the one that never got built back in 1986 or 1987. I raised a lot of money; we got pledges of over $20 million and got $4.5 million in cash, but the [ballet and opera] companies kept escalating what they wanted in the house. Ballet did not want to share dressing rooms with opera. The facility had to have the ballet rehearsal rooms in it because ballet dancers get cold running from the subway. We had previously raised money for an opera centre that had rehearsal halls and other facilities, and then [the opera company] wanted them all over again in the new building. That was a real turnoff. Finally, I got fed up with it. I eased out of it, and a lot of other donors did too.*

It's hard to imagine that a project, for which almost $25 million had been raised, was ultimately abandoned by funders because of the competing demands of the parties involved.

The Pity Plea

Studies have demonstrated that fundraising campaigns using dramatic images of those in need produce greater results.[27] The negative feelings evoked are motivational. However, assuming that all philanthropists are going to respond the same way would be a big mistake. In fact, for many, those negative images and feelings are demotivating.

In a previous chapter, we reported Eric Sprott's dislike for appeals that were what he called "sorrow based." He even went on to say:

> *Often with Africa, it's, you know, these horrible images, and I think to myself,*
> Why would I give to something where there is no hope?

Sprott perceptively recognized that guilt was the emotion being leveraged, but for him, that's just not going to work. Here is his analysis:

> *You get one of those "a child will die tonight because you're not giving," and that*
> *is not resonating with me. That's guilt. It's a big motivator. That's one of the two*
> *ways—it's either inspire or guilt, and some people will react to the guilt. Some*
> *people react to the inspiring. Me, personally, and the way I try to bring things*
> *to my board, is to inspire them [that] we can make a real difference here.*

Being Ungrateful

As we stated in our introduction, organizations often see philanthropists in one dimension—as simply a source of funding. They are lured by the financial potential. That can continue to happen even after someone has provided support. Ed Sonshine's encounter with the executive director of an organization to which he had previously made a major gift is a case in point.

> *It's a good organization. What happened was I got talking to him. At the*
> *time, it was just a few years ago. I gave him $100,000. It was a lot of money.*
> *But you know what? I really felt strongly that [the organization] could make*
> *a difference and was good. So anyways, the [director] called me up one day*
> *and says, "You know, I'd like to bring a couple of my students down to your*
> *office." It was quite fabulous. The kids were very impressive. Very clearly, the*
> *program had made a difference in their lives. And so the [director] turns to*
> *me, and he says, "So, Eddie, can we count on your support?" I said, "Well, I*
> *already gave you $100,000." And he says, "Yeah, but that was last year." And*
> *I looked at him and said, "Yeah, you can count on my support." He*
> *embarrassed me. Like the $100,000 was just nothing, and it was old news.*
> *And I never gave him another nickel. And I feel bad not giving them money*
> *because they do good work. He was very dismissive of what I thought was a*
> *pretty significant gift, and that was his mistake.*

While there may be two sides to this story, it's indisputable that Sonshine felt taken for granted. Although additional funding was likely within Sonshine's financial reach, he—like any other donor—needed to feel appreciated. Large sums can often obfuscate the small but vital emotional needs. Even though Sonshine eventually returned as a donor, that neglect, as Eddie said, was a huge mistake.

Changing the Terms

David Cynamon provided another account of what can go wrong after a gift has been made and fundraisers decide that it's time to once again visit the donor.

First, he established the magnitude of his original gift, which created a wing at a local hospital. "What I planned to give ended up being two and half times [larger]. But it is what it is, and I didn't mind. And five years later, they named the whole wing [for our family] ... very nice." Then he told us about the meeting.

> *Less than five years later, I had the head of the hospital come in and say, "We are moving your floor to the new building, and we think that [the new] floor is worth X, [now] X happens to be multiple of something that you gave, and we expect you to up [your original donation]." And they saw in my body language how disappointed and how upset I was. I swear that within five minutes, they asked if they could leave the room. I think there were three or four of them. They came back, and they apologized. I said, "I am so glad you did this because I would have ended the relationship forever." And that's a mistake they could've made with the wrong person—not gone out and thought things through and ended a long-term relationship. Not only that, [they would have] affected whatever circle that person was in. Because nobody will give major donations if they think every five years they are going to be held hostage to up it.*

This is again a case of the financial needs of an organization clouding the judgment of its fundraisers or, at best, miscalculating the donor's response. It also exposes the potential for collateral damage resulting from these interactions. The community of philanthropists is close knit. When one of them is treated inappropriately, others know about it, and that can have cascading negative impact on an organization's fundraising efforts.

Taking a Small Gift for Granted

The accepted best practice in fundraising solicitations is for the solicitor to suggest a gift amount for the donor to consider. It's not unusual for the donor to feel that the suggested amount is too high, but the fundraiser's response to that sentiment has tremendous impact on the future of the relationship. Larry Tanenbaum presented the giver's perspective.

> *I don't like those that don't appreciate even a small gift because a small gift can turn into a big gift if they are smart. So every gift is an important gift, and it should be taken that way, but there are some people who don't take it that*

way. So ... that's distasteful when it is not appreciated. The $5,000 or $10,000 gift can turn out to be $100,000 at some point in the future if the cause warrants it.

Arm Twisting

Sometimes the amount of the desired gift is communicated through means less gentle than a suggestion. That can have equally poor results. James Fleck explains.

There have been situations [where attempts were made] to shame others into giving on the basis of "I gave X, so you should give X, or you should give double X" or whatever it is. That doesn't appeal to me as an approach, and I guess I would be offended if I thought I were being pressured to give. You want to give because you want to give, not because someone's pressuring you.

Having to negotiate the amount implicitly means that the donor has agreed to make a gift. But solicitations don't always end in a yes, and the fundraiser's response to a no can also have lasting implications. Naomi Azrieli told us about one such situation when describing a solicitation to her from an academic institution.

It was a perfectly worthwhile program, and they needed money for a professor. I said, "I'm going to be very frank with you. We're on the verge of doing something with another university. And we're going to follow that through and see how it goes, and then we're going to make decisions about what we do, but I'd be happy to bring this forward to our grants committee"—which is something I don't actually say to everybody. And he said, "You know how is this going to look for me if Azrieli doesn't give?" as if to make me look bad. I said, "That's not my problem." He said, "This is going to be very awkward for me."

Naomi summed up the encounter with sage advice. "That was a bad solicitation. I was actually stunned by how bad that was. You can't always go for the hard sell. You just can't."

Unrealistic and Presumptuous Requests

Many philanthropists were bothered by those whose funding requests were completely unrealistic—even to the point of being insulting. Mark Krembil's feelings on the subject were representative.

The ones that I have not liked were the ones where they came in asking for absurd sums of money. So I may have never met you before. I know your *name. You may have a connection with my father or you are a friend of a friend. And they come here, and after a half an hour, they're asking for $10 million or for $20 million. I find that personally distasteful.*

Gerald Sheff added an urban fable to underline just how "fruitless" these requests can be.

It's like that guy selling apples for a million dollars. The guy is selling apples at an apple stand on the corner of Bay and King. The sign says Apples for $1 million, and he has a whole stack of apples. Someone comes by and says, "Mister, how many apples do you expect to sell for $1 million?" And he says, "I only need to sell one." But the fact is that you don't sell any apples for a million dollars.

Unrealistic gift requests are clearly futile, but why are philanthropists insulted by them? Philip Reichmann provided a thoughtful answer.

Probably the presumption of equals. In other words, somebody, I have no idea who they are, and they come up to you [asking for a major gift], and they think you're their best buddy. That's most offensive.

He went on to examine the solicitor's motivation for this behaviour and then added some brilliant advice.

You know some people will have to do that because they'll only get to see their target once. But it is like a salesman. You have to have strategy. If you feel like you'll only get to see this guy once and that you better ask for the big take, that's the wrong strategy. What you should be thinking about is how I turn that one visit into a first visit. The strategy should be how to get the next visit, not resign yourself that this is the only time you're going to be able to see the guy.

Souring the Experience

The face-to-face solicitation is the holy grail of fundraising. In previous chapters, we have demonstrated that philanthropists themselves recognize that an in-person meeting is most likely to result in a gift. But what's the best course of action when, for whatever reason, the philanthropist is resisting? This account by Linda Frum may provide some guidance:

The person made a big mistake because she asked me for three meetings, and this was right before the election, and I [had no time]. I kept saying, "Just tell me what it is. Just ask me. Send me an e-mail. I'll support you. Just ask me."

She said, "No, I have to meet you in person. The election is going to be over soon, and can we set up that meeting?" I finally said, "Just ask me; don't pressure me like this. What you are telling me is that you are going to ask me for something really big or make it so uncomfortable for me to say no, and I'm not interested in that. Make it easy for me to say yes." That got my back up. That was being too aggressive.

Although Frum said she would support the cause, the fundraiser was looking for the big payoff, and—in the process—ended up with nothing. After the first two rejected meeting requests, the correct decision would have been to accept Linda's offer of support and use it as the basis for building a relationship where future meetings were possible.

We wrap up the discussion with the words of Richard Ivey. In talking about the ills of the philanthropic process, he told us about a conversation he had with someone he referred to as a "huge philanthropist." This is what that person told Ivey:

You know, I really regret sometimes not having done this anonymously. I'm just bombarded. You know, I just announced this gift, and I got a call the next day from Edmonton saying, "We need you to help us with the campaign out here," and I said, "Sorry, I'm not interested." The woman on the phone said, "It's just $500,000." Stuff like that gets you after a while. They just assume because you wrote a cheque for $8 million that $500,000 is no problem, even though it is [on] the other side of the world, and you have never been there and all that sort of stuff. A lot of fundraisers hurt the profession when they do things in a sort of offhanded way.

We couldn't have said it any better. The unnamed philanthropist has effectively made the point that is at the heart of this book. Fundraisers will only be successful when they approach the philanthropist with the thoughtfulness and sensitivity he or she deserves.

Fundraising Organizations Could Do Much Better

Pareto Fundraising, an Australia-based agency, surveyed customer service levels of approximately one hundred nonprofit organizations. What they discovered was appalling.[28]

- As many as 20 percent of nonprofits do not respond when contacted by individuals interested in making a gift.

- Almost 50 percent of the charities do not pursue one-time givers for recurring or annual gifts.

- Nearly 40 percent don't have a formal method of thanking donors when they commit to annual gifts.

- It often takes charities weeks, or even months, to respond to simple requests.

- More than a few charities [mistakenly] issued receipts for donations they never actually processed.

When contacted by individuals interested in making a bequest, 31 percent didn't respond at all, 22 percent neglected to say "thank you," and 64 percent did not bother to explain the types of bequests they can leave.[29]

18

Miscellaneous is always the largest category.

—Joel Rosenberg

Too Good to Pass Up

Philanthropists told us a number of stories that didn't fit neatly into one of the subjects we chose for chapters but were so interesting or meaningful that we had to find a way to present them. So welcome to our "Too Good to Pass Up" chapter. We hope you enjoy reading these stories as much as we enjoyed hearing them.

Charles Juravinski discussed the combination of discomfort and pride that came in having his name associated with a number of health care institutions in Hamilton. The critical factor in his decision to allow his name to be used was that he hoped others would be inspired. In demonstrating how in fact the recognition has inspired others, he related this story.

> *I got a letter from a lady in very broken English. She happened to be Ukrainian, and she happened to be a widow, and she happened to have cancer. She wrote me a letter telling me how happy she was that she can get on the bus and get up to Concession Street because she lives in a lower city in Hamilton and goes to the Juravinski Hospital. And then in her broken English, she told me about her husband who died of heart disease, and she wrote, "By way, attach cheque, maybe help someone." It's twenty-five freaking thousand dollars—can you believe it? Does it inspire someone? Inspiration. A Ukrainian widow who can hardly write English taking the time and sending [the hospital] $25,000.*

Similarly, he told us about how he delighted in occasions when his giving had led others to give.

We had a campaign when every dollar someone donates, I'll put in two, up to a certain amount. I would get telephone calls where people would say to me, "Hey, big pr—k, I just cost you $2,000." "How?" I answered. "Well, I just donated $1,000." It cost me two thousand bucks. I get a kick out of that.

David Cynamon told us about how a good-intentioned gesture fell flat because it hadn't been completely thought out.

We recently had an event [for a health care organization], and all my kids were volunteers. The president of the foundation sent a really nice thank-you card to all my kids like she probably sent to all volunteers. I opened them because I open all their mail, and then I give it to them. I saw the first one was for Jesse. It had Jesse's name crossed out and handwritten, and it said, "Great job, da da da da ..." I thought, That is super. I can't wait to bring it to him. Until I opened the other two and they were exactly the same. Now I normally wouldn't have seen that, but it turned me right off. But if they really would have been personalized, that would have been really impressive.

This account from Larry Kinlin wouldn't make it into the best practices manual for fundraisers, but it probably represents something that every fundraiser wished he or she had done at some point in her career.

I'll give you another example of the United Way gift that was really funny. I was campaign chair in '72, and there was a gentleman in town who gave nothing to speak of, maybe ten bucks, like he was just terrible. He was a wealthy man, and I knew him through the Chamber of Commerce that I've been involved with for years. So I went to see him. We'll call him Sam because that's his name.

I went to see Sam, and he said, "So they're sending the big guy out, are they?" I said, "Well, we need your help." Sam replied, "What do you mean you need my help?" I said, "Well, there's twenty-six agencies. What do you think of the United Way?" His response was, "Ah, they'll take the money, and I don't know what the hell they do with it." I said, "Well, you gave us ten dollars last year. That didn't even buy the coffee for the morning." He says, "So what do you want?" I said, "Just write me a cheque. We've got to get this done. It's really important in this community."

He writes me a cheque for $100. He gave it to me, and I ripped it up, and I gave it back. Sam said, "What the hell are you doing?" I said, "That's disrespectful. That's an insult." "Really?" he replied. I said, "It certainly is. You're a big stick in this community. You're giving me $100 for twenty-six agencies. What is this? I mean, this is stupid. I mean, just stop it. We don't want it, then; we don't want anything if you can't write me a cheque of value." I was a kid. This is 1972. Now I'd play hockey against the Keons and the Brewers—I mean, I've been beat up by a lot of great guys, so I don't have to worry. "So how much do you want?" he asked. I said, "Write me a cheque." He wrote me a cheque for $10,000. That was the end of that conversation."

19

Rather than being a human, be a humanitarian.

—Kowtham Kumar K

Philanthropists Are Just People

As we reflect on the interviews that we conducted and the hundreds of hours spent reviewing, sifting, parsing, and distilling what we heard, there is one compelling common characteristic of the philanthropists that emerges. That is their humanity. We mean that in two ways. On one hand, they are humane, and it is impossible to not be overwhelmed by their generosity. On the other hand, they are very, very human with many of the same doubts, fears, foibles, and frailties that every one of us has. Simply put, they are people.

We believe that the ability to see the person in the philanthropist is the key to building meaningful relationships that lead to effective results. In this final chapter, we present some of the evidence of those human qualities and the ways in which they are significant.

The Future

A mainstay of fundraising literature is the word *legacy*. The premise is that major donors will want to make a gift that will have impact for many generations to come.

We found that for most philanthropists, as it would be for most people, the concept of a legacy is somewhat theoretical. When asked what they would like their philanthropic legacy to be, it was clear that most hadn't previously taken the time to give it much thought. They live primarily in the present.

In part, that may be a result of magnitude. The reality is that few families in Canada have wealth that even approaches that of Carnegie, Rockefeller, or even Gates. Without those kinds of fortunes, the capacity for future philanthropy may in fact be limited.

Many philanthropists have thought about how wealth will be passed to children and, in some cases, even grandchildren. But other than their philanthropy setting an example for the next generation, they are not consumed with the distant future impact of today's philanthropic involvement.

The application to fundraising is clear. One can't assume that major givers are necessarily future minded or concerned about some mythical legacy. The satisfaction that their philanthropy brings today may be all the motivation they need.

The Moment

While many, if not most, of those we interviewed had some philanthropic plan or focus, almost all prepared to listen to giving opportunities outside those bounds. The moment of opportunity could be created by a big idea, an inspirational appeal, the medical experience of a loved one, or even the education of grandchildren. Philanthropists are as subject to whim and fancy as any of us. The implications are significant.

For the fundraiser, it means that anything is possible. Given the right circumstances and motivation, a philanthropist will do the unexpected. We heard many stories of philanthropists surprising themselves by making million-dollar gifts they never dreamed of making to organizations they never planned on supporting. The premium is on creating moments that will induce a donor to give and seizing those moments in which the donor's giving impulse has been stirred.

The caveat is that just as opportunity comes, it also goes. The moment passes. The medical crisis has been forgotten. The children have left the school. There are newer, more exciting causes coming to the fore. Friends have found new avenues of involvement. Most of the philanthropists had at least one organization they had previously supported generously that is no longer a recipient of their time or money. Fundraisers can't take anything for granted. Previous support is not necessarily a predictor of future giving. That means that while stewardship is a never-ending process, the organization must be prepared for the unexpected.

The Ego

Almost everyone wants to be recognized for their efforts—the child who cleans his room, the salesperson who makes the big sale, the athlete who breaks a record. Why then would we think that philanthropists are any different? From our interviews, we can tell you that they are not. No matter what they say, you can almost bet that they want to be recognized for their giving. The more appropriate discussion may be about how and where.

Asking a philanthropist *if* he or she wants to be publicly recognized may produce a no because most people don't want to be perceived as bragging, even though they may crave the attention. It's more effective to assume that there will be some recognition and engage the philanthropist in a discussion about their comfort zone. We heard more than one account of philanthropists who, despite having previously refused any recognition, agreed to an attribution when presented with a naming opportunity that was right for them. The conversation may still be slightly uncomfortable for both the philanthropist and the fundraiser, but the result will be truly gratifying.

The Pack

Like most people, philanthropists are not lone wolves. They crave camaraderie and friendship. They are more comfortable in groups. They are susceptible to peer pressure and competition. We were surprised by the degree to which those in the philanthropic community know and associate with each other. Many declared those relationships to be one of the most gratifying aspects of their philanthropic involvement. They admitted to being influenced by each other—to giving because one of their peers is giving.

Just as few people want to be the first or only participant, philanthropists appreciate being a part of a community of givers. While they profess their dislike for dinners or events, when they are in the moment, they react like any of us would among friends or those who are like-minded. They are often surprised to have enjoyed themselves and to have found new energy and appreciation for an organization.

For the philanthropist, an organization that can demonstrate the commitment of others is both an indication of credibility and a lure of involvement. Similarly, philanthropists are often pleased to see a new generation of supporters ready to take the reigns. The fact that there are those that want to take their place is a sign that they are part of a winner—a cause that appeals to others.

The pack mentality is perfectly natural—even for philanthropists. Fundraisers need to be mindful of its influence and its implications.

The People

Philanthropists are people too. They think. They react. They feel. Like all of us, they want to be heard and appreciated. For the most part, they are also equally accomplished and benevolent. They have earned their measure of respect.

The fundraiser's prescription for success is far simpler than any system or formula. Just listen intently, treat philanthropists seriously, want them for more than their money, apologize sincerely, communicate honestly, honour commitments diligently, and show appreciation naturally.

Just as the philanthropist is a person, you must equally show your humanity. You must be real. False passion or manufactured interest will always be detectible. Authenticity is more compelling than knowledge or style.

Don't underestimate your potential or the effect you can have. If the philanthropist's vision is smaller than yours, then educate her. Motivate her though a combination of facts and emotion. Philanthropists relish the opportunity to learn and be truly inspired. Likewise, if they have vision that is larger than yours, don't be defensive or intimidated. Consider that vision and perhaps even embrace it. Let them inspire you as much as you inspire them.

Seymour Schulich provided us with an eye-opener on inspiration. During our interview with him, he referred to famed businessman and philanthropist Andrew Carnegie and told us, "This guy is the prototype. He's my idol." He then went on to talk about a group of philanthropists that are his role models. "Rockefeller, Carnegie, Annenberg—these are the big three in philanthropy that are the models that I model a lot of what I do after."

As we concluded our interview, he insisted on giving us copies of books about Carnegie, Rockefeller, and Annenberg. While we were taken aback by his generosity, we were struck by the fact that philanthropists who died almost one hundred years ago were still a source of inspiration to someone who is himself a Canadian philanthropic legend.

Billions of dollars may have been collectively donated by Canada's top philanthropists, but their greatest gift is the degree to which their giving inspires others. All of us—fundraisers, board members, donors, and volunteers—are inspired by the philanthropists' inclination to give perhaps even more than the magnitude of their giving.

Despite the fact that fundraising success is most often measured in dollars, our conclusion is that the true currency of philanthropy is inspiration.

> *Never doubt that a small group of thoughtful, committed citizens can change the world. Indeed, it's the only thing that ever has.*
>
> *—Margaret Mead*

The Superman Complex

In this chapter and throughout the book, we have emphasized the humanity of the philanthropist. We wanted to make these exceptional individuals more real. We have attempted to provide the cure for what psychologists Leif Nelson and Michael Norton have referred to as *the Superman Complex*.[30]

Studies conducted by Nelson and Norton demonstrated that when individuals considered the character traits of Superman (the action hero), they were actually half as likely to volunteer for community service. Conversely, those who merely considered the character traits of heroic individuals were four times more likely to volunteer and give back.

Effectively, thinking about Superman discouraged giving, whereas thinking about heroic individuals encouraged it. Why is this the case?

When we think of heroic individuals, we can relate to them. However, by thinking about Superman's powers, which are so far removed from our capabilities, we are discouraged from attempting to mimic them.

By presenting our philanthropists as the people they are, we have tried to step beyond their names, making them accessible and not intimidating. In that way, we hope that their example will prove to be motivational and inspiring.

20

Action is the foundational key to all success.

—Pablo Picasso

What You Can Do Tomorrow

Since actions always speak louder than words, we thought it was important to provide practical action items that will allow you to utilize the insights of Canada's top philanthropists for your benefit.

While we have organized them into those most appropriate for fundraisers, philanthropists, and board members, you would be wise to peruse all three lists. We hope you find these helpful.

Fundraisers

1. Don't make assumptions.

- Take the time to uncover the philanthropist's real motivation for previous gifts. You will then be able to present opportunities that match the philanthropist's interests. Don't either presume the philanthropist's interest or dismiss possible support based on previous giving history. Something else may have been at play, and links are not often what they seem.

- Make sure that your prospects have the capacity and/or interest in continuing to give. Not all past gifts will lead to a corresponding future gift, and you may be spinning your wheels for naught.

- Most importantly, you can't say "thank you" enough. Don't assume that they know how much you appreciate their support.

2. **Consider generational positioning.**

- You will be better equipped if you understand that there is often a different philanthropic attitude between those who created the wealth and those who are stewarding it.

- Ensure that you are prepared to accommodate next-gen donors who may only be willing to give based on having a seat at the decision-making table or some other criteria that is different from their parents.

3. **Make it face-to-face.**

- Arrange for face-to-face meetings with donors even at lower levels. Every donor will respond more generously to a personal solicitation.

- Some philanthropists' propensity to give is so strong that they can hardly say no to almost anyone in front of them. Some even have a policy that they'll give a token gift to anyone they see.

- A good (or better) alternative to the personal meeting is inviting the philanthropist to visit your organization, giving them the opportunity to "fall in love" with what you are doing.

4. **With a donor, be in the moment.**

- Be prepared to capitalize on emotional situations. Emotion can be the key to unlocking a philanthropist's true giving inclination. Context and circumstance can be more important than the perfect solicitation. Respectfully and thoughtfully take advantage of the opportunity.

- Be on the lookout for opportunities to ask donors to increase their gifts. It's possible to be an effective partner to the philanthropist by suggesting a larger gift commitment.

- Capitalize on the impact of fundraising events through prompt follow-up. Those who were in attendance may be motivated to give or do more. These are powerful (and generally overlooked) sales opportunities.

5. **Leverage a donor's business interests.**

- Always be prepared to align your solicitation with the philanthropist's corporate or marketing goals. It will give the philanthropist more buckets to pull from and increase your chances of creating a win-win scenario.

- Don't assume that it will require less effort to obtain corporate gifts. Many philanthropists do distinguish between corporate and personal giving, but the underlying inspirations remain. People still have to be personally motivated to support the cause.

6. **Like it or not, people give to people, not causes.**

- The "right person" is different for every prospect. There is no formula. Give great consideration to who is most likely to close the deal.

- The right person isn't necessarily you. Know when to take yourself out of the picture and let someone more influential to the individual be the deal maker.

- Stack the deck by having a number of influential people involved in any campaign. Everybody knows somebody.

7. **Make it easy to get involved.**

- Make involvement attractive and easy, and identify involvement opportunities that are uniquely tailored to the philanthropist's strengths and interests.

- For the philanthropist, time is more valuable than money. Having said that, consider asking the philanthropist first for his or her time and only later for the money. The payoff of involvement can be far greater, as significant dollars often follow.

8. **Don't underestimate the value of research.**

- Research is an ongoing necessity and essential to the stewardship process. That especially includes good listening.

- Be very cautious how much of your research you reveal until you find out how the philanthropist feels about being the subject of it.

9. **There is rarely a downside to asking.**

- Always be asking. The worst mistake is one of omission.

- Beyond that, the wise fundraiser knows that even a no can be the basis for relationship building.

10. Nobody is looking for more problems.

- Make solicitations solution based and positive. Focus on what will happen with greater support. Simply expounding on the need may not be motivating. No one is looking for more problems, stress, or guilt.

- Every "ask" should empower the giver to build a better community, world, or society.

Philanthropists

1. Be generous with your insights.

- An offer of advice as opposed to money is not necessarily a consolation prize. Often, worthy advice is more valuable than a cheque.

- Offering advice to the professional also allows you the opportunity to see how he or she responds, and it can provide insight into what it would be like to work with the individual.

- Honest feedback can also give the fundraiser a much greater chance of success in the future.

2. Help fundraisers make the "ask."

- Don't waste their time, and help them avoid wasting yours. Ask them what exactly they are looking for from you as quickly as possible. It will help clear the tension and focus on the purpose of your meeting.

- If your answer to a solicitation is no, don't delay in letting the fundraiser know or ignore her due to the discomfort of saying no. Procrastinating will only lead the fundraiser on and ultimately waste everyone's time.

3. Encourage risk taking.

- No business plan is perfect and risk proof. The same is true of any worthwhile and meaningful charitable endeavour. Recognize that even in philanthropic organizations, great gains don't come without risk.

- Accept the prospect of failure, and encourage learning from mistakes.

4. Research your solicitors.

- Through research, you can determine if the representatives of an organization are the type of people you'd want to be involved with and help you to avoid those with whom you do not want to be involved.

- Research may also provide some insight into just how committed the solicitor is to a cause. For example, if you're being approached by a professional who has jumped from organization to organization, that person may not be there to ensure that your gift has its intended impact.

5. Always think long term.

- Spreading out your gifts (even to the same organization) and giving gradually may be better than the quick major gift.

- Generally, it pays to start small and grow your commitments. This will take risk out of a singular major investment and allow you to get truly acquainted with the organization.

6. You can inspire the vision for the organization.

- Don't underestimate your ability to help an organization see a bigger picture and affect greater change.

7. Inspect what you expect.

- It would often help for you to regard your gifts as your investments. Make sure that you are clear about what you consider to be appropriate ROI.

- If you care deeply about efficiency and effectiveness in the organization(s) that you support, you will have to get involved.

- Do your own due diligence, and ensure the people and organization you are supporting are consistent with your values. Remember, while you can often exit your financial investments, especially those in publicly traded markets, you cannot exit your charitable gifts—at least, not without potentially embarrassing repercussions.

- It's okay to be demanding. Feel comfortable in asking organizations to challenge themselves.

8. Take advantage of synergies.

- There is no harm or shame in considering how your charitable interests align with your business interests.

- Some of the most successful companies have sophisticated corporate social responsibility programs that do exactly that. Philanthropists with private business interests can take a page out of these companies' playbooks, as it will often help focus, enhance, and sustain their giving.

9. Limit guilt offerings.

- Don't compromise your passion for philanthropy by enduring unpleasant arm twisting from causes that don't resonate with you.

- Have a budget for "token" gifts for those organizations, and don't waste your energy and resources supporting that which you resent supporting. While a "token" gift is relative, it should not represent a major portion of your philanthropic giving.

- Have a reciprocity strategy.

10. Follow the golden rule.

- In the donor-solicitor relationship, there is an apparent imbalance, where the donor appears to hold the upper hand and leverage. Resist the urge to view yourself as more important than the organizational fundraisers or other staff members.

- True philanthropists aren't simply generous with their wallets but also generous with their hearts. Having the generosity of spirit to treat everyone as you would like to be treated is the pinnacle of philanthropy, and the richness of that dynamic will make your involvements more enjoyable.

Board Members

1. Embrace your "difficult" supporters.

- Difficult donors are often the most responsible for the improvement of your institution. Resist the urge to discount them, and know that the stress of their exactingness can often pay off.

- Philanthropists are often looking for a partnership. Embrace it, and take advantage of what they bring to the table—aside from money.

2. Don't rely on the (marketing) collateral.

- Not one philanthropist we interviewed ever made a decision to support a cause on the basis of any piece of marketing material—yet most expected you to have it.

- On one hand, the material has to be informative and attractive. On the other hand, it can't be over the top.

- Consider personalization of marketing collateral as a way of making it more relevant to the donors.

- Make sure your website is attractive, up to date, and communicates effectively.

3. Don't bank on reciprocity for getting the gift.

- The quid pro quo is a principle that most businesspeople accept and understand. It can be a useful tool in opening doors but won't necessarily "close the sale."

- Reciprocity is about people's sense of mutual obligation and has little to do with the organization. It's not the best way to create lasting relationships.

- While philanthropists accept the principle of reciprocation, many do so begrudgingly. Be careful that your organization is not tarnished by the negative feelings that can be generated.

4. They want you—not the professionals.

- Philanthropists will say that they want introductions to come from peers, colleagues, and friends, not professionals.

- Having said that, don't abandon your professionals and development staff to do solicitations alone.

5. Provide special treatment. It's expected.

- Notwithstanding their discomfort about asking for it, donors do feel entitled to receive some extraordinary treatment, and it can cement a relationship. Let them know it's okay to ask.

- Provide perks in a way that doesn't compromise the donor's pride or the integrity of the organization.

6. Mind the downside.

- Philanthropists understand that projects don't always go as planned. What they look for is honest and effective communication.

- Just because a donor doesn't revoke a gift doesn't mean you haven't left a bad taste in his mouth. Manage the gift and the relationship.

7. It's all in the details.

- Attention to detail is important in every interaction with the donor and can be key to developing and enhancing the relationship.

- There is no escaping the need for accountability. Be prepared for it. Anticipate and be proactive with the metrics for success.

- Vision and detail go hand in hand. The ability to provide metrics has the potential to enhance the vision.

8. The lack of passion can undermine an otherwise perfect pitch.

- Passion is a critical differentiator. It can set you apart from other causes.

- Passion can't be faked. Be sure to allow the philanthropist to interact with those who truly love and believe in what they are doing.

- Your passion and personality can compensate for the most dramatic mishaps.

- The success of the board is often highly correlated with the passion of the professionals and lay leaders involved.

9. If you accept the gift, you accept the vision.

- Once you accept a gift based on the philanthropist's vision, you assume ownership of that vision and responsibility for its implementation.

- Embrace and nurture the unique vision of the philanthropist, as long as it doesn't contradict the broader mission of the organization.

10. Challenges are inspirational.

- Such challenges as matching gifts, grant deadlines, stretch goals, and "chal-lenge" gifts can be the catalyst to great results. While embracing challenges doesn't guarantee success, odds are that you will accomplish more by doing so.

- Internal organizational challenges should not be swept under the carpet. Be prepared to disclose and confront them. Failing to be transparent will only exacerbate the impact of whatever skeleton in the closet you're attempting to hide.

Appendix

Biographies of the Philanthropists

As you have likely discerned by now, at the core of the philanthropic mind is the belief and understanding that philanthropy is all about the people. With this in mind, we devote a special section to the people who make philanthropy in Canada what it is. Here are some of the philanthropists we interviewed extensively for *The Philanthropic Mind*

Shreyas Ajmera

Shreyas Ajmera is the owner of Seenergy Foods Inc., the IQF food-processing company established in 1994 for the development of top-quality, nutritious, yet affordable gourmet foods. An accomplished inventor, Ajmera owns several patents, including one for a process for preparing individually frozen pulses and one for an improved packaging tray. Bringing together a combined passion for all things historical and a keen sense of philanthropic responsibility, Ajmera is a major contributor to the Royal Ontario Museum, sitting on the ROM governing board, the Donor Relations and Recognitions Task Force, and Renaissance ROM Campaign Cabinet, and—with his wife, Mina—making a major gift to the museum which established the Shreyas and Mina Ajmera Gallery of Africa, the Americas, and Asia-Pacific.

Naomi Azrieli

Dr. Naomi Azrieli, Chair and CEO of the Azrieli Foundation, as well as President of Canpro Investments, cannot recall a time when her family was not involved in philanthropic efforts. With her late father, a Canadian-Israeli architect, designer, and developer, Azrieli has for several years supported numerous organizations, initiatives, and programs in architecture, design, and the arts; education; Holocaust commemoration and education and Jewish community; and scientific and medical research. These include, among others, providing intensive tutoring, social skills training and parenting tools to encourage academic retention for at-risk learners with the Azrieli Institute for Educational Empowerment; supporting graduate students, post-docs and junior faculty at Israeli universities and promoting academic excellence and leadership through the Azrieli Fellows Program; backing the collection, archiving, publication, and distribution of memoirs and diaries of Holocaust survivors in Canada by the Holocaust Survivor Memoirs Program via the Azrieli Series of Holocaust Survivor Memoirs; and supporting scientific research and education at various instions, including the Weizmann Institute of Science, Hebrew University in Jerusalem, Technion – Israel Institute of Technology, and with various partners, including Brain Canada, the Canada Institutes for Health Research, the International Development and Research Corporation and the Israel Science Foundation.

Lawrence Bloomberg

At the drafting of this book, the distinguished businessman and philanthropist Lawrence Bloomberg had just been named the Ryerson University chancellor. He comes to this position with a robust résumé of professionalism and giving combined. A Member of the Order of Canada, and the Order of Ontario, Bloomberg has supported, sponsored, and made endowments to the University of Toronto's Lawrence S. Bloomberg Faculty of Nursing, Mount Sinai Hospital's Frances Bloomberg Centre for Women's and Infants' Health, Concordia University's Lawrence Bloomberg Chair in Accountancy, the Lawrence Bloomberg Wing at the Schulich School of Business, the Wharton School of Pennsylvania's Lawrence S. Bloomberg Fellowship, the Bloomberg Manulife Prize for the Promotion of Active Health at McGill University, and the Terry Fox Run across Canada for cancer awareness campaign, among many others. He is a founder and director of the MaRS Discovery District. Bloomberg is the chairman of BloombergSen, a member of the board of directors of the National Bank of Canada, an advisor to National Bank Financial, and has been inducted into the Investment Industry Hall of Fame.

Brendan Calder

Former CEO, chair, and president of CIBC Mortgages (1995–2000) and former chair of the Peter F. Drucker Foundation and TIFF, Brendan Calder is currently entrepreneur-in-residence; strategic management professor of the award-winning second-year MBA course, GettingItDone; chair of Desautels Centre for Integrative Thinking and the founding chair of the Rotman International Centre for Pension Management at the Rotman School of Management, Calder is also an ICD.D corporate director and continues to make major philanthropic contributions. For his efforts spanning more than three decades, he has been awarded numerous honours and awards, including induction into the Canadian Mortgage Hall of Fame in 2004 and over ten excellence in teaching awards.

Tony Comper

Tony Comper is the immediate past president and CEO of BMO Financial Group. He began his career at BMO in 1967 and was appointed president in 1990. Comper, who sits on several boards, along with his late wife, Elizabeth, founded FAST, a new initiative to combat anti-Semitism in Canada, and serves as co-Chair of the capital campaign for the Royal Conservatory of Music. In 1998, Comper received the Human Relations Award from the Canadian Council of Christians and Jews. In 2003, he received the Award of Merit from B'nai Brith Canada. He holds an honorary LLD from the University of Toronto, an honorary DHL from Mount Saint Vincent University, and an honorary DLitt from the University of New Brunswick, among others. Comper and his wife also received the Scopus Award from the Hebrew University of Jerusalem.

Martin Connell

The thirty-year executive head of Conwest Exploration Company Ltd., founded by his grandfather Frederick M. Connell in 1938, Martin Connell developed the business, seeing its evolution from mining to oil and gas exploration and development. He then expanded his repertoire to include the founding, with his wife, Linda Haynes, of ACE Bakery in 1993 and Calmeadow, the micro-entrepreneurial support organization established in 1983 to provide credit and financial services in developing countries. Serving in several philanthropic capacities, Connell has served on several boards. Because of Connell's decades of support in the non-profit sector, he has garnered several prestigious honours and awards, which include honorary doctorates from five universities; appointment as an Officer of the Order of Canada in 1998; the United Nations Canada Pearson Peace Medal, conferred upon Connell in 1994; and—in celebration of his longtime philanthropic service to the Toronto Community Foundation, where he was board chair until 2011—the establishment of the Martin Connell Spirit of Philanthropy Award in June of that year.

Sydney Cooper

Former president and CEO of Pitts Engineering Construction Ltd., one of Canada's leading infrastructure construction companies, Cooper is president of Toril Holdings Ltd., is director of Clairvest Group Inc., and runs—along with his wife and family—the family foundation. Besides also sitting on several boards, Cooper has been a longtime supporter of several deserving institutions. As a result, several scholarships, chairs, and buildings have been established in his or his wife's name, including S. C. Cooper Sports Medicine Clinic at Mount Sinai, the Sydney C. Cooper Chair in Business and Technology, and many others.

David Cynamon

Former Toronto Argonauts and Liberty Grand co-owner David Cynamon has been making his mark since he was a teenager. The entrepreneur, named one of Canada's Top 40 under 40 by the *Globe and Mail* and recognized as Ernst & Young Entrepreneur of the Year in 2002, Cynamon is also an accomplished sportsman and has made numerous contributions to sports in the nonprofit sector, including a recent five-year gift to the Tennis Canada's Tennis Matters campaign for high-performance athletic development. Cynamon's philanthropy extends beyond sports, as well, and with his wife, Stacey, he has contributed significantly to, among others, Toronto's Hospital for Sick Children, where a chair sits with the name David and Stacey Cynamon Clinical Scholar in Pediatric Neuroscience Endowment Fund; renovation of Mount Sinai Hospital's tenth-floor postnatal unit, also named for the Cynamons; the Edmonton Jewish Foundation; and the United Jewish Appeal. For his support, Cynamon has been honoured with several awards, including the B'nai Brith Foundation Award of Merit, conferred upon him in 2007.

Aubrey and Marla Dan

Aubrey Dan is a Canadian businessman and philanthropist as well as a Tony Award–winning producer and impresario. He is founder and president of Dancap Private Equity Inc., Dancap Global Asset Management, Dancap Catering, and Dancap Productions Inc. Besides numerous other accolades, in 2008, Aubrey received an honorary doctorate of laws from Assumption University.

Marla Dan is not only dedicated to raising their two beautiful children, Alyse and Myles, but is also deeply active in the community. Marla currently serves as the national president of Canadian Hadassah-WIZO (CHW), one of Canada's leading Jewish women's organizations with over ten thousand members.

Together, the Dans have made major contributions that include the Sunnybrook Foundation for its women's and babies' program, now called the Aubrey & Marla Dan Program for High-Risk Mothers & Babies; the University of Western Ontario's Social Science department (which now features the program named Dan Management and Organizational Studies); Baycrest Centre (where a building has been named the Reuben Cipin Healthy Living Community in Toronto); the Judy Dan Wound Care Centre; and the University of Toronto's Leslie Dan Faculty of Pharmacy.

Leslie Dan

A former pharmacist and current leading service, business, and health care professional, Leslie Dan established Canada's largest prescription drug company, Novopharm Ltd. (now Teva Canada), then the equally successful Novopharm Biotech (later named Viventia). Leslie Dan has continuously contributed to research, development, and education initiatives, projects, and programs, making gifts to establish the University of Toronto's Leslie L. Dan Pharmacy Building and Leslie Dan Faculty of Pharmacy and making significant contributions to the Holocaust memorial and education centre, Yad Vashem. In 1985, he also founded CAN-MAP, which provides medicine and aid to developing countries. For these and many more philanthropic efforts, Dan has been granted three honorary doctorates; was made Member of the Order of Canada in 1996; was awarded the Order of Ontario in the same year; and, early in 2010, was presented with a special lifetime achievement award for his philanthropic support of promoting bilateral trade between Canada and Israel.

Carlo Fidani

Carlo Fidani is the third-generation owner of the construction, development, and management company Fidani and Sons, now known as Orlando Corporation. The real estate developer is also cofounder of Canadian Motorsport Ventures, which he, racing legend Ron Fellows, and transportation industrialist Alan Boughton established upon purchase of Mosport International Raceway in 2011. Fidani has contributed several million dollars to the Princess Margaret Hospital Foundation, with a $5 million "challenge" donation; to the University of Toronto, for construction of the Terrence Donnelly Health Sciences Complex; the Centre for Addiction and Mental Health; and the Carlo Fidani Peel Regional Cancer Centre, which, as a redevelopment project for research in bioinformatics and computational biology, won the 2006 Community Scale Significance Award and the 2008 Design Excellence Award.

James Fleck

James Fleck is Rotman emeritus M. Wallace McCutcheon professor of Business Government Relations at the University of Toronto, co-founder of the Faculty of Administrative Studies at York University, and has served as President of the Art Gallery of Ontario Foundation, member of the board for the Canadian Museum of Civilization Corporation, secretary of the cabinet and the chief executive officer at the Office of the Premier, and Deputy Minister of Industry and Tourism for Ontario. Chairman of several firms, including Business for the Arts, the Harvard-educated Fleck is founding CEO of Fleck Manufacturing Inc., the appliance-wiring-system company he ran until its sale in 1994. Much of Fleck's work involves his tireless philanthropy, which, over some thirty-five years, has included the Fleck Tanenbaum Chair in Prostatic Diseases and the Prostate Centre at Princess Margaret Hospital and the Canadian Arts Summit, among others. A Ford Foundation fellow since 1964 and a Companion of the Order of Canada since 2014, Fleck has won several more honours and awards for his cultural philanthropy, including the 1996 Public Policy Forum Testimonial Dinner Award for Distinguished Service to Canada, the 2008 Edmund C. Bovey Award, the 2009 Angel Award, and the 2009 Ramon John Hnatyshyn Award.

Linda Frum

Senator Frum is an accomplished politician, author, award-winning filmmaker, and active philanthropist. A former contributing editor to *Maclean's* and a former columnist for the *National Post*, Frum is also the author of two Canadian best sellers, *Linda Frum's Guide to Canadian Universities* (1987) and *Barbara Frum, A Daughter's Memoir* (1996) and the documentary *Ms. Conceptions* (1995), which was named Best Social-Political Documentary Program and awarded the 1996 Gemini Award, the 1996 NEMN Competition Silver Apple, and the 1995 IDA Awards Silver Certificate. Frum has won several awards for her active community volunteerism, including the 2010 Golda Meir Leadership Award and the 2006 Canadian Council of Christians and Jews Human Relations Award, the latter an honour shared with her husband, Howard Sokolowski. Her philanthropy extends across Canada, and she sits on several boards, including the United Jewish Appeal Women's Division, the Canada Israel Committee, the Ontario Arts Council, and the Canadian Club of Toronto. She is also Vice Chair of the board of governors of Upper Canada College and is a member of Senate of Canada—an appointment assigned her in August of 2009 by Prime Minister Stephen Harper.

Harry Gorman

Real-estate developer Harry Gorman is president and board director of Wycliffe International Design Group, the Toronto-based firm established in 1994. An avid supporter of projects, programs, and initiatives for the health care industry, Harry has—with his wife, Sara—made numerous significant contributions, including donating to the Holland Bloorview Kids Rehabilitation Foundation; volunteering at Baycrest; serving on the board of the Toronto General & Western Hospital Foundation; and establishing the Hy & Bertha Shore and Harry & Sara Gorman Award. For these and many other philanthropic efforts, Gorman has received several honours and awards, including appointment as honorary member of the Star of David Society and of the Jewish Legacy Society, both with the Jewish Foundation of Greater Toronto in appreciation of his establishment of a PACE gift and/or large permanent endowment fund of, respectively, $200,000 or $500,000 or more.

Gerald Halbert

Former dentist and businessman for several decades, Gerry Halbert spends countless hours devoted to philanthropic efforts. These include, among others, advising for SportsSmart Canada and ThinkFirst Canada; acting as one of the 175 key leaders in the University of Toronto's Great Minds Campaign; serving as Co-chair and campaign executive committee member for the Krembil Neuroscience Centre at Toronto Western Hospital, member of the Mount Sinai Hospital board of governors, and board member for the Toronto General & Western Hospital Foundation; and serving as both President and Chair for UJA Federation of Greater Toronto. Also an advisor on numerous committees, including the Krembil Neuroscience Centre Brain Campaign, Gerry Halbert has been an accomplished fundraiser for several other campaigns, including for the development of the Wolfond Centre for Jewish Campus Life at the University of Toronto, for the University Health Network Campaign, and for the establishment of research chairs for both the University of Toronto and the University Health Network. For his significant contributions, Gerry Halbert has received several honours and awards, including an honorary doctorate from Canadian Friends of the Hebrew University and appointment as member and officer of the Order of Canada in 2001 and 2002 respectively.

Jay Hennick

Founding CEO and former president and chair of FirstService Corporation, Jay Hennick began his professional career founding Toronto-based Superior Pools; and merged the company with American Pool Enterprises, and formed the subsidiary, FirstService Residential Management. Hennick practiced as a corporate lawyer, working as a partner with Fogler, Rubinoff LLP; has been named Ontario's Entrepreneur of the Year for Consumer Services; has won Canada's Entrepreneur of the Year award for creative service integration; and was named Canada's CEO of the year by *Canadian Business Magazine*. Co-founder (with his wife, Barbara) of the Jay and Barbara Hennick Foundation, his philanthropy spans the spectrum from business and law to health care, education, and medical research and reaches across the globe with many contributions, including launching the global social giving campaign Everyone Gives (2012); the donation to and naming of the Hennick Centre of Business and Law; the Jay and Barbara Hennick Foundation for Medical Research at Mount Sinai Hospital; and the Jay Hennick JD/MBA Program at the University of Ottawa Law School. Hennick was awarded an honorary doctorate from York University in acknowledgment of his many years of contributions.

Richard W. Ivey

Richard W. Ivey brings forty years of law practice and business leadership roles in real estate, logistics, and packaging to his current work in real estate development and management. Current Chairman of the board of Ivest Properties Ltd. And MaRS EXCITE, and past Chair of the Canadian Institute for Advanced Research and Livingston Group Inc., among others, Ivey also sits on several more boards, including Canada Colors and Chemicals Ltd., the Toronto Foundation, the Ivey Foundation and the MaRS Discovery District. For these and numerous other contributions to the community, education and research and innovation, he was made a Member of the Order of Canada in 2006.

Hal Jackman

Hal Jackman is best known as the former lieutenant governor of Ontario, but he also served as chairman of the board for, among several others, the Empire Life Insurance Company and National Trust Company; he was chancellor of the University of Toronto (1997–2003); and he has a long history as a patron of the arts. In 1995 he established the Lieutenant Governor's Awards for the Arts. As well,

Jackman has made significant contributions to education and the arts, having served in several capacities on numerous boards—including for the Art Gallery of Ontario, the Council for Business and the Arts, Ontario Heritage Foundation, the Royal Ontario Museum, and Shaw Festival and Stratford Foundation Festival Funds—and donating, as the largest gift ever made to a university, $30 million to establish University of Toronto's Jackman Humanities Institute. For his many contributions, Jackman has been awarded nine honorary doctorates and has received numerous awards, including the 2008 Edmund C. Bovey Award and appointments as both Member and Officer of the Order of Canada.

Aditya Jha

Chairman and board member of many start-up and turn-around businesses, Aditya Jha has been in the chocolate manufacaturing business at Karma Candy Inc.; e-business and product marketing at Bell Canada; is founder of the software company Isopia Inc. and cofounder of the software company Osellus Inc. & Osellus Asia Pacific Co. Ltd.; and has been a longtime philanthropic supporter of education and entrepreneurship. Founder of POA Educational Foundation (2001), Jha is active in advising, supporting, and funding several individuals, institutions, and initiatives, including those to whom he has made large endowments for academic scholarships: George Brown College and Ryerson University, Trent, and York Universities, among others. Jha has served on numerous boards, including for the UNICEF Canada India HIV/AIDS campaign and the Ryerson University capital campaign; and, working with the office of the Grand Chief of Nishnawbe Aski Nation, Ryerson University and Trent University, has been an influential leader in Canada's aboriginal communities. For his tireless efforts, he has received several accolades, awards, and honours. These include an honorary doctorate from Ryerson University (2009), a citation as one of *Toronto Star/Canadian Immigrant* magazine's Top 25 Canadian Immigrants of 2010, and appointment as Member of the Order of Canada in 2012.

Donald K. Johnson

With an MBA from the Ivey Business School and four years split between two businesses—Canadian General Electric in Toronto and Federal Electric Corporation on the DEW line in the Canadian Arctic—accomplished entrepreneur and celebrated philanthropist Don Johnson began work as an investment research analyst before moving on to become President of Burns Fry, Governor of the Toronto

Stock Exchange, Chairman of the Investment Dealers Association of Canada, and Vice Chairman of BMO Nesbitt Burns. Semi-retired, Johnson is now very active in the not-for-profit sector, sitting on a number of advisory boards, including for the Richard Ivey School of Business, the Toronto General & Western Hospital Foundation, the Council for Business and the Arts in Canada, and United Way of Greater Toronto, among others. In addition, Johnson has a lead role in lobbying the federal government to remove tax barriers for gifts of publicly listed securities to registered charities. He has received numerous awards and honours, including, among others, the Association of Fundraising Professionals' 1997 Outstanding Volunteer Award, the 1998 Richard Ivey School of Business Distinguished Service Award, the 1999 Arbor Award for Outstanding Volunteer Service to the University of Toronto, and appointment as Member and as Officer of the Order of Canada.

Charles Juravinski

Canadian businessman and philanthropist Charles Juravinski is principally known as the founder and owner of the Flamboro Downs racetrack and the co-benefactor—along with his wife, Margaret—of the Juravinski Hospital and Juravinski Cancer Centre in Hamilton, Ontario. Juravinski relocated to Hamilton, Ontario, motivated by job opportunities arising from wartime industry, and began work in the construction industry, so by 1958, along with his brother-in-law, he had founded WilChar Construction based in Hamilton. Following his retirement, he and his wife, Margaret, made considerable endowments to the City of Hamilton and McMaster University, permitting the establishment of a new state-of-the-art cancer care facility at the former Henderson Hospital, now renamed Juravinski Hospital.

David Kassie

David Kassie is Chairman of the Board of Canaccord Genuity Group Inc. David was Principal, Chairman and CEO of Genuity Capital Markets [November 2004 to May 2010] at which time Genuity was acquired by Canaccord Genuity Financial. He is the former Chairman and Chief Executive Officer of CIBC World Markets and the Vice Chairman of CIBC [from 1979 – 2004].

Mr. Kassie has extensive experience as an advisor, underwriter and principal. He sits on a number of corporate boards and is on The Advisory Board of Omers Ventures. Mr. Kassie is actively involved in community and charitable organizations and is on the Boards of Baycrest Health Sciences (currently Vice-Chair and incoming Chair), the Ivey School of Business, the Toronto International Film Festival Group and formerly on the Board of the Hospital for Sick Children as well as the Shoah Foundation. Mr. Kassie was the 2009 B'nai Brith Canada Award of Merit recipient. Mr. Kassie was a member of the McGill Men's Basketball Team from 1972 to 1977 and was inducted into the newly formed McGill Redmen Basketball Wall of Honour in 2014.

Mr. Kassie holds a B.Comm. (Honours) in Economics from McGill University, 1977 and an MBA from the University of Western Ontario, 1979.

Warren Kimel

Warren Kimel is the CEO of Fabricland, the largest retail chain of fabric stores across Canada. Besides his numerous professional achievements, Kimel is exceptionally active in the community, his volunteer roster including work for the UJA Federation, Beth Sholom Synagogue, United Synagogue Day School (USDS), and the B'nai Brith Lodge, Toronto Freedom. He currently serves as chair of the Baycrest Centre Foundation Board. For all these efforts, Kimel has been recognized with the 2006 Beth Sholom Humanitarian Award, among many others. Kimel has had the passion for giving from early on, and through his present role in the Kimel Family Foundation, he has seen to the fulfilling of the wishes in his sister's will with the creation of Baycrest's Elkie Adler MS Clinic, provider of the innovative rehabilitation that Kimel champions. With his wife, Debbie (Freeman) Kimel, became the benefactor of the Kimel Education Centre at the Community Hebrew Academy of Toronto and has supported several programs and events, such as Toronto's Ashkenaz Festival; and continues the family foundation practice of discrete giving that reaches back to medicine, medical machines, and health care.

Larry Kinlin

President of Larry Kinlin & Associates Inc., Larry Kinlin has been a licensed advisor in the financial services sector for forty years. He and his firm are associated with Schwaben Financial Counsel Inc., where Kinlin, a member of the advisory group, assists in the provision of long-term financial risk and needs analysis and related estate advisory services. Also a longtime philanthropist who has practiced charitable giving using life insurance, Kinlin is a contributor to several organizations and individuals, including serving on the board for the Hospital for Sick Children and on the boards of four other charitable organizations. Perhaps best known is his donation history and ongoing support of the Larry Kinlin School of Business at Fanshawe College in London, Ontario.

Julia Koschitzky

With the family, founders of IKO, Julia Koschitzky has served as a model of Canadian philanthropy. She learned the value of family, Jewish community, and giving throughout her early years, and began her first philanthropic ventures as she raised her own family, first assisting with outreach programs for the UJA Federation system and then extending her efforts to the Centre for Jewish Studies at York University, as well as Keren Hayesod. Julia has served in several capacities on several advisory boards, including for the Jewish Agency for Israel, the Keren Hayesod World Board of Trustees, the United Jewish Communities of North America, and the Pincus Fund for Jewish Education of the Jewish Agency. Koschitzky has earned numerous honours and awards, including the 1997 Ben Sadowski Award for outstanding dedication to the Toronto Jewish Community, the 1997 Israel Goldstein Prize for outstanding service to the Keren Hayesod, Toronto's UJA Business and Professional Women's Division 1990 Woman of Valour Award, the 1994 Canadian Zionist Federation Jerusalem Award, the 1999 Volunteer Service Award of the Province of Ontario conferred by the lieutenant governor; and, in 2003, an honorary doctorate from Yeshiva University.

Mark Krembil

Former co-owner of the national Canadian retail company Lewiscraft and senior systems engineer for EDS Canada, Mark Krembil is President of the Krembil Foundation, established in 2002 to support medical research and childhood education. He is currently serving on several boards, including NoNO Inc.; Brain Canada, where he chairs the Audit and Finance Committee; Toronto General & Western Hospital Foundation, where he chairs the Research Committee; the Centre for Addiction and Mental Health (CAMH) where he chairs the Research Committee; and is the Lieutenant Governor In Council (LGIC) member of the University of Toronto's Governing Council. With the family foundationand wife, Stacey, Krembil has contributed to several initiatives and endeavours, including the Krembil Discovery Tower at the University Health Network; the Krembil Chair in Neuroscience at Toronto Western Hospital; ThinkFirst Foundation of Canada, the expansion of ThinkFirst's sports injury prevention programs; and Mount Sinai Hospital, to support computational biology and modern genomic research.

Joe Lebovic

Joe Lebovic made his start in Canada working for the family in the lumber industry. By 1953, he had established, with his father and brother, Wolf, the commercial and industrial land development and housing construction business, Lebovic Enterprises Ltd. Lebovic has for many years been involved in numerous philanthropic endeavours: he has served in several capacities on numerous boards, including for Ner Israel Yeshiva College, the Scarborough Board of Health, the Foundation Office of Scarborough Hospital, and Scarborough Centenary Hospital; and he is now on the board of governors for B'nai Brith, Canada, and on the board of the Baycrest Centre, JDC, UJA Federation, the Markham Stouffville Hospital, Mount Sinai Foundation, Mount Sinai Hospital, and Israel Bonds. Besides earning several awards for his professional work, the major contributor to the Joseph and Wolf Lebovic Community Campus has received many honours for his charity work—among them the 2005 Spirit of Jerusalem and the Canada Medal for the 125th anniversary of the Confederation of Canada by the governor general of Canada.

Eric Lindros

Winner of the 1995 Lester B. Pearson Award, Eric Lindros is an accomplished hockey player, playing on the Oshawa Generals, the Quebec Nordiques, the Philadelphia Flyers, the New York Rangers, the Toronto Maple Leafs, and the Dallas Stars. Lindros has also led such teams as the Oshawa Generals to Memorial Cup victory (1990); has captured the title of Most Outstanding Player in the OHL, which earned him the Red Tilson Trophy (1991); and has been named Player of the Year by the CHL. Lindros retired from hockey in 2007. That same year, he donated $5 million to create the Lindros Legacy Research building at the London Health Sciences Centre, which houses the Fowler Kennedy Sport Medicine Clinic where Lindros had received excellent care by exceptional doctors. Lindros continues to dedicate extraordinary amounts of time to a wide variety of charities and causes.

Kelly Meighen

A graduate of Western University, where her father, the late Colonel Richard Dillon, was the first dean of engineering, Kelly Meighen has had a professional career that has seen her in roles for Beech, Shepell & Associates; General Foods Inc.; and the Ontario government. Today, she is president of the T. R. Meighen Family

Foundation. For more than three decades, Meighen has been heavily involved in community service and charitable giving. Besides serving the Meighen Foundation and Western University, she has served on numerous boards and is a major supporter of Evergreen at the Brickworks, Stratford Shakespeare Festival, Toronto's Centre for Addiction and Mental Health, and Upper Canada College, among others. For her many years of volunteer service, Kelly Meighen has won awards, including the Association of Fundraising Professionals 2008 Outstanding Philanthropist Award.

Gil Palter

An accomplished entrepreneur, Gilbert Palter has worked at Clairvest Group Inc., McKinsey & Company, Morgan Stanley, and Smith Barney; has served as Chairman of Aurigen Reinsurance Corporation, BFI Canada (now Progressive Waste), BreconRidge Corporation, Continental Alloys & Services, Farley Windows, Hair Club Group, Specialty Commerce Corporation, and Stephenson's Rental Services; and has been a member of numerous boards, including those of Alliance Films, Center for Diagnostic Imaging, Eurospec Manufacturing and Tooling, Mitel Networks Corporation, Trimaster Manufacturing, Tunnel Hill Reclamation, and Xantrex Technology. Founder, CEO, and Managing Director of Eladdan Enterprises and Eladdan Capital Partners, Palter is also Co-Founder and Chief Investment Officer at EdgeStone Capital Partners Inc. A member of the Young Presidents' Organization, Palter was named as one of Canada's Top 40 Under 40 in 2003; and was a recipient of the Ernst & Young Entrepreneur of the Year Award in 2006 and 2007. Gil is very committed to a number of philanthropic causes. He has been involved with and the impetus behind many initiatives within the Jewish Federation movement and recently served as the campaign co-chair for the UJA Federation of Toronto.

Philip Reichmann

Given the online honorarium as a Canadian business icon, the reputedly very private Philip Reichmann is equally known for his extensive philanthropy. Mr. Reichmann is co-founder of ReichmannHauer Capital Partners, which—together with Frank Hauer—he began in 1993 after fifteen years of experience as a commercial leasing representative at Olympia & York Developments Ltd. Besides having a rich history of involvement in such projects as the development of New York City's World Financial Trade Center and London's Canary Wharf, he is active in several charitable causes; and with a special interest in hospital foundations and Jewish education, Mr. Reichmann has a seat on the board of Mount Sinai Hospital, the human rights organization, the Friends of Simon Wiesenthal Center for Holocaust Studies, and others.

Larry Rosen

Taking over for his father, Harry, in 2005, eldest son Larry Rosen is chairman and CEO of Harry Rosen Inc. With a bachelor of arts, a master's, and a law degree, he practiced corporate law before joining the firm and took on several positions before heading Harry Rosen. A supportive volunteer outside of business, Rosen is a member of several boards, including the Ivey Advisory Board, the Ivey Entrepreneurship Advisory Council, and the Princess Margaret Hospital Foundation board of directors. He is at the helm of the Harry Rosen United Way campaign and was key in launching Harry's Spring Run-Off, which has raised millions for cancer research.

Seymour Schulich

A co-conceiver of the practice of royalty payments for the mining industry, Seymour Schulich went from a position at Shell Oil Company to Vice Chairman and President of Beutel, Goodman & Company Ltd. to Director and Merchant Banking Chair of Newmont Mining Corporation as well as owner of Canadian Oil Sands Trust. Besides being an accomplished entrepreneur and author of *Get Smarter: Life and Business Lessons* (2007), Schulich is a celebrated philanthropist, giving major support to numerous institutions of higher education both in Canada and in Israel. Among many others, these include support leading to the creation, naming, and/or renaming of the Schulich School of Business at York University, Schulich School of Engineering at the University of Calgary, and Schulich School of Law at Dalhousie University, among several others. He is also the creator and benefactor of the Schulich Leader Scholarships that promote academic excellence in STEM subjects both in Canada and in Israel. Schulich is also a major donor to the Sunnybrook Health Sciences Centre. Seymour Schulich has been honoured for his many major national as well as international contributions. He has been the recipient of honorary doctorates from six universities; has been inducted into both the Canadian Mining Hall of Fame and the Canadian Business Hall of Fame; and he was appointed Member, and subsequently Officer, of the Order of Canada.

Gerry Schwartz

Co-founder of the Canadian Council for Israel and Jewish Advocacy and Can-West Global Communications Inc. and major fundraiser for the Liberal Party of Canada, the entrepreneur known as "Canada's Henry Kravis" is the CEO of the private equity firm Onex. A major supporter of local, national, and international projects, programs, and peoples, Schwartz—along with his wife, Heather Reisman—is a benefactor of Toronto's Mount Sinai Hospital. He established the HESEG Foundation that provides scholarships to lone soldiers in Israel; he has made donations leading to Saint Francis Xavier University's Gerald Schwartz School of Business and to a successful University of Waterloo exchange program for the Canadian university and Israel's University of Haifa; and his generous support of University of Toronto Faculty of Law and Rotman School of Management has resulted in the JD and MBA academic gold, silver, and bronze medals being named after him. Schwartz has also been the recipient of several awards, including, among others, the 2005 Ernst & Young Entrepreneur of the Year Award and the appointment as an Officer of the Order of Canada in 2006.

Issy Sharp

Founder of the Four Seasons Hotels and author of *Four Seasons: The Story of a Business Philosophy* (2009), Isadore "Issy" Sharp is a man of many major accomplishments and just as many admirers. He is a director of the Bank of Nova Scotia and a director of Clairvest Group. He serves philanthropically on several boards, including the Mount Sinai Hospital and Canadian Unity Council; and he is founding director of the Terry Fox Run and Governor of the Canadian Council of Christians and Jews. In addition, he has provided corporate and personal support to the Four Seasons Centre for the Performing Arts, Hebrew University of Jerusalem, and the Ontario College of Art and Design, among others. His generosity has led to the creation of several buildings, departments, events, and items in his and his family's name, and he has received numerous honours and awards, including Companion to the Order of the Canadian Business Hall of Fame (2008), Ernst & Young Entrepreneur of the Year (2005), a Lifetime Achievement Award from the International Hotel Investment Fund (2009), a Lifetime Achievement Award from the International Luxury Travel Mart (2011), honorary doctorates from Ryerson and York Universities, and Officer to the Order of Canada (1993).

Gerald Sheff

Gerald Sheff is Co-Founder and Honourary Director of Gluskin Sheff + Associates Inc. Mr. Sheff graduated from the School of Architecture at McGill University in 1964, and received a Master of Business Administration degree from the Harvard Business School in 1971. Mr. Sheff is a Governor Emeritus of McGill University and a member of both its Investment Committee and the Committee to Advise on Matters of Social Responsibility. He is a trustee of the Art Gallery of Ontario Foundation and a member of its Investment Committee, and a member of the Board of Directors of the Canadian Centre of Architecture. He also serves on the Advisory Board of the Scotiabank Giller Prize and is a lay bencher of the Law Society of Upper Canada.

Honey Sherman

With her husband, Bernard (Barry) Sherman, Honey Sherman created the Apotex Foundation to support charitable causes nationally and internationally. Sherman has served in several philanthropic capacities, including leadership roles within the UJA Federation, the Jewish Foundation of Greater Toronto, Mount Sinai Hospital, the Baycrest Centre for Geriatric Care, and York University. For her many major contributions to the communities of Canada and the United States, Sherman has received several honours and accolades, including, among others, Association of Fundraising Professionals' 1996 Outstanding Philanthropist Award, which she received with her husband, Barry.

Alex Shnaider

Former commodities trader Alex Shnaider is co-founding director of the private company, Midland Group. Shnaider, who is also known for his partnership with Donald Trump for Toronto's Trump International Hotel and Tower, is owner of Midland F1 Racing (formerly Jordan Grand Prix). Perhaps lesser known is Shnaider's penchant for charitable service, which he practices dutifully with his wife, Simona. Among many others, he has contributed generously to the Hospital for Sick Children; Mount Sinai Hospital, where his support created the Alex and Simona Shnaider Research Chair in Thyroid Oncology; Sunnybrook Hospital; and Toronto General & Western Hospital, where he has donated to the Peter Munk Cardiac Centre and where his support created the Alex and Simona Shnaider Cardiology Inpatient Unit.

Gary Slaight

President and CEO of Slaight Communications, Gary Slaight has given much to the community. His broadcasting company, Standard, has been credited with reinventing Canadian radio; is founder of Slaight Music; sits on the board of the academy of Canadian Cinema and Television; is an inductee to the Canadian Music Industry Hall of Fame in 2005; and four times has been named the CMIA Broadcast Executive of the Year. The head of the Slaight Family Foundation, he has also relentlessly supported numerous causes, initiatives, and campaigns. In 2014, the Foundation made a landmark gift of $50 million to be distributed equally among five health care institutions in Toronto – Toronto General and Western Hospital, St. Michaels Hospital, Sunnybrook Health Sciences Centre, the Centre for Addiction and Mental Health and Mount Sinai Hospital. That was followed in 2015 by a $7 million commitment – $1 million to each of 7 Canadian NGOs including the Stephen Lewis Foundation, War Child, Free the Children, Right to Play, Human Rights Watch, Partners in Health Canada and World Vision. With the Foundation he has contributed to CARAS's MusiCounts and to the Dixon Hall Music School; and he has established the Slaight Family Scholarship for students of Berklee College of Music. As member of several boards—including the Canadian Academy of Recording Arts and Sciences, and the National Arts Centre Foundation—Gary Slaight has received several awards, including the Award for Outstanding Community Service by an Individual Broadcaster, the 2010 Humanitarian Spirit Award, the 2012 Walt Grealis Special Achievement Award and was made a member of the Order of Canada in 2014.

Eddie and Fran Sonshine

Together, Eddie and Fran Sonshine have become a potent charitable force—among other philanthropic accomplishments, fund-raising for numerous causes and groups, serving on several boards, and establishing one of the first Toronto Jewish Foundation legacy funds. For such generous giving, the couple has received tribute several times over. They have been the honourees at Baycrest's 2008 Tribute Gala, in 2003 by the Canadian Society for Yad Vashem, receiving the 2003 International Spirit of Jerusalem Award from State of Israel Bonds, and being honoured at the 2006 Jewish National Fund Negev Dinner.

Eddie Sonshine

A lawyer who practiced law for fifteen years, Eddie has served as a Director for Royal Bank of Canada, Chesswood Group Ltd., and Cineplex Inc., and has served as founder and CEO of RioCan Real Estate Investment Trust. Eddie is also a former chairman of the United Jewish Appeal Campaign in Toronto and is a director of Sinai Health System. In addition to the many awards he has received with his wife, Fran, Eddie Sonshine has been appointed as Queen's Counsel and as Member of the Order of Ontario.

Fran Sonshine

Fran Sonshine, consummate community service volunteer and benefactor, has been Chair of the Baycrest Foundation and President of Toronto Hadassah-WIZO, and currently serves as National Chair of the Canadian Society for Yad Vashem, national honorary Vice President of Hadassah-WIZO, and a board member of CIJA, Mount Sinai Hospital, and UJA Federation's Jewish Foundation. She is also one of five members of the National Holocaust Monument Development Council, raising funds for the monument to be completed by 2016. Fran has received numerous awards and honours, including the Queen Elizabeth II Diamond Jubilee Medal, the State of Israel Bonds Canada's Golda Meir Leadership Award, the UJA 2011 Ben Sadowski Award of Merit, the UJA 2010 International Kipnis-Wilson/Friedland Award, the UJA Shem Tov Award, and the Toronto Hadassah-WIZO 1996 Volunteer of Distinction Award.

Eric and Juliana Sprott

Eric Sprott and his daughter Juliana Sprott run the Sprott Family Foundation—founded by Eric, his wife, Vizma, and Juliana and her sister, Larisa, in 1988—to serve national and international human needs. Through the foundation, Eric and Juliana have made major contributions to these communities, including making one of the largest private donations ever made to the University Health Network's Department of Surgery.

Eric Sprott

Founder of Sprott Asset Management and Sprott Securities Inc., Eric Sprott earned a chartered accountant certification from Carleton University, was a research analyst with Merrill Lynch, founded his first business, the institutional brokerage firm SSI, in 1991, and divested SSI to the employees of the firm and started Sprott Asset Management in 2000. With the establishing of the family foundation, Eric became a renowned philanthropist, supporting causes through donations to Daily Bread Food Bank, Carleton University, the Ottawa Hospital Foundation, the United Way, University Health Network, and the YMCA, among many others. Besides his many awards for visionary business practices, including the 2006 Ernst & Young Entrepreneur of the Year Award for Ontario and the 2012 Most Influential Hedge Fund Manager Award, Eric Sprott has been honoured several times for his support through the years, including being elected fellow of the Institute of Chartered Accountants of Ontario to recognize his demonstration of both outstanding career achievements and community service.

Juliana Sprott

Toronto-born and -educated Juliana Sprott worked in sports broadcasting before becoming president of the Sprott Family Foundation. Sprott brings passion and compassion to her philanthropy, investing in philanthropic workshops like the one she and colleagues attended in New York in February of 2007 and in foundation giving, which has included her cherished contributions to such nonprofit organizations as Daily Bread Food Bank, Second Harvest Canada, and the Stop Community Centre and such support campaigns as the 2007 Annual Daily Bread Food Bank Gala and the 2007 Virgin Unite Canada.

Larry Tanenbaum

Cornell-educated Larry Tanenbaum is co-owner of the Toronto Maple Leafs, Toronto Raptors, Toronto FC and Toronto Marlies and serves as the chair of Maple Leaf Sports & Entertainment. He is a Governor and member of the Executive Committee of the NHL (Toronto Maple Leafs), the NBA (Toronto Raptors), and Major League Soccer (Toronto FC). He is a member of the Board and Executive Committee of the Hockey Hall of Fame in Toronto, Ontario. He is currently chair and CEO of Kilmer Van Nostrand Co. Ltd.

He is rigorously involved in community philanthropy and has contributed to several efforts, initiatives, and institutions including landmark support of the Lunenfeld-Tanenbaum Research Institute at Mount Sinai Hospital where he also serves as Co-Chair of the Research Board. Tanenbaum has lent his support to UJA's Tomorrow Campaign, Mount Sinai Hospital, the Centre for Israel and Jewish Affairs (of which he is a founding member), Brain Canada, the Miller Thomson Foundation, Baycrest Centre for Geriatric Care, Montreal Neurological Institute, the Schulich School of Business, Right to Play and the University Council at Cornell. For his efforts, Larry Tanenbaum has received several honours, including an honorary doctorate from St. Michael's College at the University of Toronto and Officer of the Order of Canada.

Fred Waks

Accomplished retail developer Fred Waks is the President and CEO of the Trinity Development Group and the former President and COO of RioCan Real Estate Investment Trust. He is also—with his wife, Linda—a tireless supporter of projects, programs, initiatives, and institutions both in Canada and Israel, having served as Chair and Co-chair on several different boards, including United Jewish Appeal, the Israel Emergency Campaign during the Second Lebanon War, UJA Federation's Israel emergency campaign, UJA Federation, and the Forest Hill Jewish Centre's capital campaign. Also creating the Fred and Linda Waks Chair in Jewish Studies at the University of Western Ontario, Waks has often been acknowledged for his active involvement in the Jewish community at home and abroad with several awards and accolades, including the more recent Jewish National Fund 2012 Negev Dinner in his honour.

Brett Wilson*

Brett is an entrepreneur, philanthropist and a Western Canadian icon. He the co-founder of FirstEnergy Capital, one of the leading investment banks servicing global participants in the energy sector. Brett is also Chairman of Canoe Financial, a privately owned investment management firm with over $1.5 billion in assets. Brett has spent three years on the hit CBC TV show, Dragons' Den, where he established himself as the lead deal-making "dragon." In addition, he acted as the host of *Risky Business*, and most recently completed his first book, *Redefining Success: Still Making Mistakes*. As a noted philanthropist and self-described "capitalist with a heart," Brett has sought to inspire, engage, and lead the business community into seeing corporate social responsibility as an opportunity. To this end, he has raised tens of millions of dollars for Canadian charities. He is also the founder of the W. Brett Wilson Centre for Entrepreneurial Excellence, has been recognized as "Alberta's Business Person of the Year," "Calgary's Person of the Year," as "Nation Builder" by The Canadian Youth Business Foundation, and received an Honorary Doctorate of Laws from Royal Roads University. He is a member of the Order of Canada and recipient of Saskatchewan's Order of Merit.

Brett Wilson's quotes are adapted from his book, Redefining Success: Still Making Mistakes.

We have done our utmost to ensure the accuracy and timeliness off the information in these biographies. We apologize for any errors or omissions.

Endnotes

1. Adam Grant, *Give and Take*, 20–21; Shalom H. Schwartz and Anat Bardi, "Value Hierarchies across Cultures: Taking a Similarities Perspective," *Journal of Cross-Cultural Psychology* 32 (2001): 268–290.

2. Peter Grant, *The Business of Giving: The Theory and Practice of Philanthropy, Grantmaking and Social Investment* (New York: Palgrave, 2012), 12.

3. *Canadian Press*, September 16, 2008.

4. Rene Bekkers and Pamala Wiepking, "A Literature Review of Empirical Studies of Philanthropy: Eight Mechanisms That Drive Charitable Giving" in *Nonprofit and Voluntary Sector Quarterly* 40, no. 5 (2011).

5. Ken Stern, *With Charity for All: Why Charities Are Failing and a Better Way to Give* (New York: Anchor, 2013).

6. The Next Gen Donors research project; 21/64 (www.2164.org), and the Dorothy A. Johnson Center for Philanthropy (www.gvsu.edu).

7. Grey Matter Research, "Heart of the Donor," Russ Reid Company, March 2011, http://www.greymatterresearch.com/index_files/Parental_Influence.htm.

8. Kent E. Dove, *The Art and Science Of Personal Solicitation*.

9. S. M. Cutlip, *Fund Raising in the United States: Its Role in America's Philanthropy* (New Brunswick, NJ: Rutgers University Press, 1965), 6.

10. Joe Chidley, "Seymour's Way," *Canadian Business*, December 9, 2009.

11. Ken Stern, *With Charity For All: Why Charities Are Failing and a Better Way to Give,* (Tornto, Random House of Canada, 2013), 140.

12. Reynold Levy, *Yours for the Asking: An Indispensable Guide to Fundraising and Management*, 136–137.

13. Adam Grant, *Give and Take, 241*; Francis J. Flynn and Vanessa K. B. Lake, *"If You Need Help, Just Ask: Underestimating Compliance with Direct Requests for Help,"* Journal of Personality and Social Psychology 95 (2008): 128–143.

14. Adam Grant, *Give and Take*, 156–157; L. J. Walker and J. A. Frimer, *"Moral Personality of Brave and Caring Exemplars,"* Journal of Personality and Social Psychology 93 (2007): 845–60, doi:10.1037/0022-3514.93.5.845.

15. Barbara Oakley, Ariel Knafo, and Michael McGrath, eds., *Pathological Altruism* (New York: Oxford University Press, 2011).

16. Adam Grant, *Give and Take, 182*; Arthur C. Brooks, *Who Really Cares* (New York: Basic Books, 2006); *"Does Giving Make Us Prosperous?"* Journal of Economics and Finance 31 (2007): 403–411; and Gross National Happiness (New York: Basic Books, 2008).

17. Baruch Lev, Christine Petrovits, and Suresh Radhakrishnan, "Is Doing Good Good for You? How Corporate Charitable Contributions Enhance Revenue Growth" (September 1, 2008), http://ssrn.com/abstract=920502.

18. Herb Greenberg, "How Values Embraced by a Company May Enhance That Company Value," *Wall Street Journal*, October 27–28, 2007; Reynold Levy, *Yours for the Asking: An Indispensable Guide to Fundraising and Management*, 75–76, 158.

19. Netta Weinstein and Richard M Ryan, "When Helping Helps: Autonomous Motivation for Prosocial Behavior and Its Influence on Well-Being for the Helper and Recipient," Journal of Personality and Social Psychology 98 (2010): 222–244.

20. Mark R. Kramer, "Catalytic Philanthropy," *Stanford Social Innovation Review*, 2009.

21. Ken Burnett, *The Zen of Fundraising: 89 Timeless Ideas to Strengthen and Develop Your Donor Relationship*, 77–78.

22. Olga Klimecki and Tania Singer, "Empathic Distress Fatigue Rather Than Compassion Fatigue? Integral Findings from Empathy Research in Psychology and Social Neuroscience" in Pathological Altruism, ed. Barbara Oakley et al.

(New York: Oxford University Press, 2011), 368–384; and Richard Schultz et al., "Patient Suffering and Caregiver Compassion New Opportunities for Research, Practice and Policy." Gerontologist 47 (2007): 4–13.

23. Ken Stern, *With Charity for All: Why Charities Are Failing and a Better Way to Give* (New York: Anchor, 2013).

24. Ken Stern, *With Charity for All: Why Charities Are Failing and a Better Way to Give* (New York: Anchor, 2013).

25. Hilary Howard, "Philanthropist Takes Hands-On Approach to Giving," *New York Times*, November 11, 2011.

26. Charles Bronfman and Jeffrey Solomon, *The Art of Giving: Where the Soul Meets a Business Plan* (San Francisco: Wiley, 2010).

27. Deborah A. Small and Nicole M. Verrochi, *The Face of Need: Facial Emotion Expression on Charity Advertisements*, Journal of Marketing Research Vol. XLVI (December 2009), 777–787

28. Ken Burnett, *The Zen of Fundraising: 89 Timeless Ideas to Strengthen and Develop Your Donor Relationships* (San Francisco: Wiley, 2006).

29. *Ken Burnett,* The Zen of Fundraising: 89 Timeless Ideas to Strengthen and Develop Your Donor Relationships *(San Francisco: Wiley, 2006).*

30. *Leif D. Nelson and Michael I. Norton, "From Student to Superhero: Situational Primes Shape Future Helping,"* Journal of Experimental Social Psychology *41, no. 4 (July 2005): 423–430.*

CPSIA information can be obtained
at www.ICGtesting.com
Printed in the USA
LVHW111459300819
629527LV00006B/52/P